THE UNOFFICIAL
Millennium
Companion

THE COVERT CASEBOOK
OF THE
MILLENNIUM GROUP

VOLUME ONE

THE UNOFFICIAL
Millennium
Companion

THE COVERT CASEBOOK
OF THE
MILLENNIUM GROUP

VOLUME ONE

N. E. Genge

Century · London

Published by Century in 1997

1 3 5 7 9 10 8 6 4 2

Copyright © N. E. Genge 1997

First published in the United Kingdom in 1997
by Century Limited
Random House, 20 Vauxhall Bridge Road,
London SW1V 2SA

Random House, Australia (Pty) Limited
20 Alfred Street, Milsons Point,
Sydney, New South Wales 2061, Australia

Random House New Zealand Limited
18 Poland Road, Glenfield, Auckland 10, New Zealand

Random House, South Africa (Pty) Limited
Endulini, 5a Jubilee Road, Parktown 2193, South Africa

Random House UK Limited Reg. No. 954009

A CIP catalogue record for this book is available
from the British Library

Papers used by Random House UK Limited are natural,
recyclable products made from wood grown in sustain-
able forests. The manufacturing processes conform to the
environmental regulations of the country of origin

ISBN 0 7126 7833 6

Typeset in Officina Sans and Concorde

Design & page make-up by Roger Walker

Printed and bound in the United Kingdom by
Butler & Tanner Ltd, Frome and London

DEDICATION

For Peter,
With love, and thanks.

ACKNOWLEDGEMENTS

Working on *The Unofficial Millennium Companion, Volume One* was often a disturbing, even frightening, experience made possible by the support and dedication of some incredible people. With my deepest appreciation, my thanks to:

Penda MacIntyre, Dean Cant, Mark Purcell and James Penner, The Group that helps shed light on The Millennium Group, as well as the Society of Former Special Agents of the Federal Bureau of Investigation for their invaluable assistance in separating fact from fiction.

Elaine, Paul, Frank, James, Colin, Walter and Roy, the most special of Special Agents for their unending support of my various projects, for sharing their wealth of experience in all aspects of criminal investigation, and for answering all the hard questions.

Larry Pinter for providing practical examples of graphology in action – and for a new paranoia about leaving hand-written notes on the refrigerator!

The wonderful people working diligently at Victim's Services divisions across the United States and Canada, especially to Elsa Martel who was kind enough to introduce me to so many of them, and to 'Lidia W.' whose generosity let me see these folks in action. Good luck.

Paula Monroe for her guidance in obtaining an amazing assortment of criminal interview transcripts – and for answering questions at three in the morning!

John Sainsbury for stepping in to bring order out of the chaos inherent in nearly eight thousand pages of research notes, transcripts and interviews. Thank you!

Maria Rejt, Kate Elton and Sue Lyne at Century for their ongoing efforts in making this project the best it can be, for the hours spent haggling with everything from seemingly possessed trans-Atlantic facsimile machines to taxation forms, and for remembering that six hour time difference!

Ling Lucas, who, in addition to being a terrific agent, remains one of the nicest people it has ever been my pleasure to work with. And to Ellen van Wees, who, in addition to helping keep Ling sane, provides her clients with ample help and general good cheer.

And, as always, to Peter and Michael for their unflagging support and for constantly rearranging their lives to accommodate the madness I optimistically call my 'schedule'. Love You.

Contents

Introduction

Dozens of television programs debut each fall, and every one of them is hyped to the limit of its demographics and budget, every one of them is 'The Season's Smash Hit' even before a real world audience gets to plunk down on the couch and vote in the age-old way – with their remote control.

Even in that environment, however, the *Millennium* launch was over the top. Billboards, buses, the sides of buildings, anything big enough to carry the 'wait – worry – who cares' mantra was covered in *Millennium* advertising. Fox simulcast a big screen opening of the première episode over the Internet, tossed a party in Scotland where a few lucky viewers saw the theatre release of *Millennium: The Pilot*, and made record sales of an unseen product to Great Britian and Spanish Pay TV. Fans of *The X-Files* were screaming in frustration as the première of 'Chris Carter's other show' was put off until 25 October, 1996, the latest start for any one-hour drama that season.

And I felt heartily sorry for Chris Carter's team.

On the other side of all that hype was a degree of industry pressure totally out of kilter for what was, essentially, a new cop show. Things were getting tense on any number of fronts. When Fox announced its plan to shift *The X-Files* out of its amazingly successful Friday night slot, the fan base everyone had hoped would transfer to *Millennium* went wild. Thousands of messages poured across the Internet in a matter of hours, with a significant proportion of them claiming they'd been rooked, that they weren't about to play into such obvious viewer manipulation, and that they fully intended to boycott the new program!

Just weeks later, *Millennium* was in the paper press's headlines, for forcing the shutdown of the numerous Web pages that had been springing up mushroom-like across the country in anticipation of the première. While Fox has some justification, namely the appropriation of its copyrighted material for use in unsanctioned websites, Fox's flat declaration that it intended to be the only source of information on its programing smacked just that bit too much of 'Big Brother' and the entire incident left even more potential fans with that sour taste in the back of their throats.

Then, imagine everyone's surprise, at both Fox and NBC, to discover they'd both independently developed programs that, on the face of it at least, appeared to be virtually identical in concept! With the introduction of NBC's *Profiler*, starring Ally Walker, weeks before *Millennium* was to air, it was inevitable that viewers would begin wondering just who copied who. *Millennium* had become an also-ran instead of a unique entry into the viewing wars. Comparison was inevitable.

And, over in the corner, the critics were sharpening their pencils...

It's a sad fact that, while everyone loves a winner, no one, especially critics, wants to be seen following the crowd. That in itself seemed reason enough to take potshots at a program that was so eagerly awaited. Dozens of reviewers received advance copies of the pilot episode... and the results weren't exactly what everyone had hoped for. Sure, some critics took the time to comment fairly, supporting their opinions with hard facts, but it's controversy that really makes headlines and any number of reviewers were panning a show they claimed 'used violence to pander to the lowest common denominator' or strictly for its 'shock value'. One reviewer wrote a three-page slam article – only to later admit he'd just seen part of the tape because he was 'inundated by dozens of different show tapes at that time of year'!

Still, for all that, *Millennium* finally premièred in the United States with some of the best numbers for the season.

The next week, the ratings that had looked so promising took a nosedive.

Television is a little like banking. If you tell people you think income from their current investments is going to fall, they'll move their investments, which in turn affects rates on the reduced pool remaining, and, in a self-fulfilling cycle, income earned from the remaining investment falls. Substitute Nielsen ratings points for investment income and you discover a great truth about television – at least half a program's value is in people's perceptions of how well the program is doing, regardless of how 'good' the show may be.

As the numbers circulated, a certain degree of gloom, independent of the show's content, began to hover over *Millennium*. Would this be the season's big flop after all?

Well, luckily, even number-crunchers understand that all figures are *relative*. Sure, there'd been a sizeable drop-off since the première, and, yes, there had been any number of programs consistently scoring higher, but put into the context of a first-season show, which would have to grow its own audience, *Millennium* wasn't doing that badly. In fact, what numbers it was pulling were in all the right demographics, that lucrative market between 18 and 49 years old. And, like it or not, television programs serve exactly one purpose – to sell advertising time.

How did *Millennium* stack up?

Well, next to the two programs it is most compared to, *The X-Files* and *Profiler*, you'd be hard pressed to choose a winner between *Millennium* and *Profiler*, but, surprise! Plotting each program's numbers for the first twelve episodes head-to-head quickly reveals some of the rather startling truths out there.

How will this dark, powerful, cutting-edge morality play do? Predictions like that require more than crystal balls, however, as each taut, nerve-racking episode airs, it's rapidly becoming obvious that *Millennium* is no 'serial killer of the week' program. Nor have the concerns about its level of onscreen violence ever really panned out. Instead, these talented people have somehow contrived to create yet another intriguing and challenging world for viewers to play in – and, slowly but steadily, those all important numbers are showing that viewers really will come back to a show that leaves them with things to think about after the credits roll.

And, hopefully, this companion volume will, by illustrating how well the fictional world of *Millennium* conforms to our own, deepen your appreciation for some truly remarkable television.

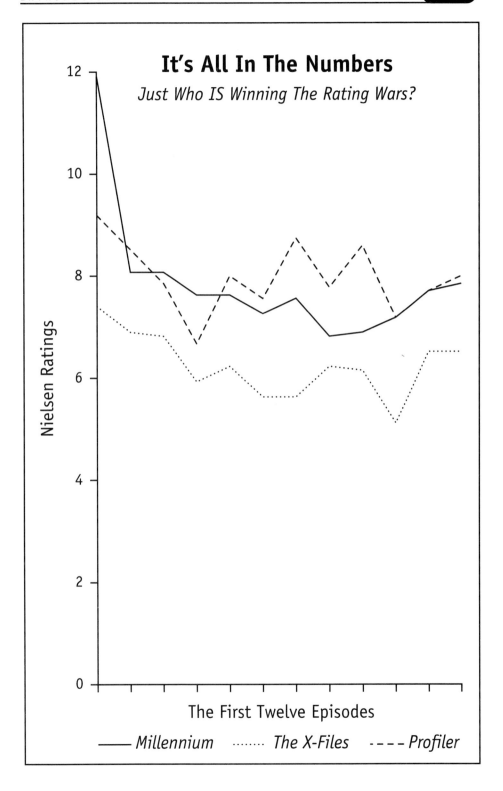

It's All In The Numbers

Just Who IS Winning The Rating Wars?

Nielsen Ratings

The First Twelve Episodes

—— Millennium ·········· The X-Files - - - - Profiler

CASE FILE: *Millennium:* 'The Pilot'

CASE SYNOPSIS:

Moving back to Seattle isn't the idyll Frank had hoped for.
Even before the Blacks unpack their cartons, Frank Black is
drawn to the case of a murdered stripper – and an M.O. with
which he's all too familiar. When the killer's personal mixture
of poetry and prophecy seems destined to make him not only
a repeat offender but a full-fledged serial killer, Frank and the
Seattle Police Department must come to a wary understanding – before the killer turns Seattle's gay community into his
permanent hunting grounds.

KEY CITATION:

LT ROBERT BLETCHER   This Millennium Group ... They
                      really believe all that stuff?
                      Nostradamus and Revelations?
                      The destruction of the world?

FRANK BLACK   They believe we can't just sit back
                      and hope for a happy ending.

VITAL STATISTICS:

Original US Airdate:	25/10/96
Production Number:	4C79
Written by:	Chris Carter
Directed by:	David Nutter

Regular/Recurring Cast:

Lance Henriksen	Frank Black
Megan Gallagher	Catherine Black
Bill Smitrovich	Lt Bob Bletcher
Brittany Tiplady	Jordan Black

Guest Cast:

Stephen James Lang	Detective Geibelhouse
Paul Dillon	The Frenchman
Terry O'Quinn	Peter Watts
Don Mackay	Jack Meredith
Mike Puttonen	Pathologist Massey
Jared Blancard	Young Man at Ruby Tip
Kimm Wakefield	Young Woman
Jim Thorburn	Coffin Man
John Destry	Driver on Bridge
Liza Huget	Nurse
Jim Filippone	Chopper Pilot

Death Toll:	1 female victim, decapitated
	1 male victim, burned alive

CASE HISTORY:

NOSTRADAMUS: PROPHETIC POET?

If 'bloody glove' was the catchphrase for the two-year stretch of the Simpson trial, then terms like 'millenniarism', 'eschatology', and 'postapocalyptic' are rapidly becoming the favoured soundbites for the remaining years of the decade. No fewer than 37 books appeared in 1996 alone, all purporting to explain the 'Millennium Effect'; pointed evidence of how drastically the meanings have shifted since they were last popular, sometime during the 990s.

Back then, the end of the world, at least in mostly-Christian Europe, was nothing more nor less than the ultimate confrontation between God and Satan. Today's theories are more convoluted, extending beyond the limited scope of religious literalists. While Christian theologic theory continues to drive the millennial debate forward, non-biblical prophets and prophecies have also found their way into the mix.

> **BLOOPER!** The sound crew got a little too enthusiastic on this episode. Adding the standard 'car engine starts' sound effect, when there was already exhaust pouring out from under the Killer's car, might be considered … overkill.

Among the most famous of the apocalyptic poets, and some would say the most eerily accurate, is one Michel de Nostredame, perhaps better known as Nostradamus. Nostradamus, while amusingly precocious as a child and a gifted scholar as an adult, demonstrated absolutely nothing unusual in his beliefs or perceptions until he, like most of the biblical prophets, was almost forty. Of course, a lot had changed for Michel de Nostredame in those forty years. A noted, if somewhat unorthodox doctor (he refused, against current common sense, to bleed his patients), he enjoyed a relatively privileged position. He married an acknowledged local beauty. He had two children of whom he is reputed to have been extraordinarily fond. Life was good. And, during this time, there was nothing to indicate he dreamt or envisioned anything out of the ordinary.

Then the Black Death returned in force. Michel de Nostredame had actually spent most of his early practice among plague victims, with as much success as any of the more experienced physicians of the day. This time would be different, however. The disease struck hard among his patients, then claimed both his children and his wife. In addition to the personal tragedy this marked in de Nostredame's life, it killed off his thriving practice. Who, after all, wanted to be treated by a physician who couldn't protect his own family?

And what physician, watching his patients dying, despite his best efforts, could not believe he was living in humanity's last days?

Once again imitating biblical prophets, Michel de Nostredame 'wandered in the wilderness', in this case the countryside of Provence. He emerged some time in 1544 and began his fight against the Plague once more, this time in Marseilles. Also in 1544, within months of de Nostredame's arrival, Marseilles was struck by floods. The floods, disrupting the city's primitive waste disposal system, washing bodies and excrement into the homes of people living near the waterways, created the perfect location for even more virulent outbreaks of the Plague. De Nostredame stuck it out, however, saving many that might otherwise have ended up in the mass graves and burial pyres. Only when the disease seemed to have moved on once again, but with the twin disasters very much a part of his world view, did he also move on, this time to Salon.

It was in Salon, after marrying Anne Ponsart Gemelle, a widow of independent means, that Nostradamus began writing widely, heavily influenced by his reading and research on mysticism and occult topics. In 1550, at 47 years of age, he began publishing his own work and, in 1555, the first edition of his early *Prophesies* appeared. The rest followed with relative speed. Called 'Centuries' for the 100 four-line verses, each section, with some variation, contained the *Prophesies* purported to reveal future events up until the year 3797.

So, if his prophecies contain references to a future as distant as 3797, why would his work have been tied up with a 'Millennial Effect' supposed to self-destruct in 2000? Simply put, it was because Nostradamus, 'to protect the innocent' and himself, admitted he'd fudged the timeline, mixing events out of order to prevent future scoundrels from anticipating any given event and capitalizing on it. The prophecies are, therefore, cast 'in terms that are cloudy rather than plainly prophetic'. And, at a time when 'magic' was a crime punishable by some rather unpleasant forms of execution, he was known to obscure his work in symbolism, puns, satire and metaphor.

Students of his work, citing the number of quatrains they have already matched to major world events, suggest that the end may be much closer than 3797, certainly within the rather broad parameters set out as the end of the millennium as defined in biblical references.

Of course, as his detractors are as quick to point out, Nostradamus's prophecies, in the best prognosticostic tradition, could, charitably, be called 'vague', if not, as some claim, 'pure nonsense'. The language mix, French, Provençal, Latin, Greek, even a smattering of Italian, doesn't make literal translations to any language easy. English, with its mongrel heritage, is perhaps the hardest of languages for translators and the English translations of the *Prophesies* are frequently even more obtuse than the originals.

Still, some of the quatrains seem to hit amazingly close to the mark.

IV-89

> Thirty of London will conspire secretly
>
> Against their King, the enterprise on the sea:
>
> He and his courtiers will have a distaste for death,
>
> A fair King elected, native of Friesland.
>
> (Omarian translation)

Whether or not there were exactly thirty conspirators remains unknown. However, it's probably as good an estimate as any, conspirators being notoriously difficult to count at any time; but it is historical fact that William III, King of England was undoubtedly both fair and a native of the Netherlands' Friesland. He stayed King of England by turning the tables on James II who'd been conspiring for the throne and, in gathering the signatures of those still loyal (or paid to be loyal) William's men spent several months at sea between England and Holland. It was that list of signatures, delivered fresh off the boat, that convinced James II his attempt was doomed to failure. A fine set of coincidences? Perhaps, but when Nostradamus jotted that quatrain in about 1557, there was no possibility of a successor to the English throne coming out of Holland.

Still more seemingly specific is:

I.35

>The young lion shall surmount the old
>One martial field in duel man to man.
>Two breaks at once, eyes pierced in cage of gold,
>Death shall come hard as only dying can.
>
>(from the French, by Peter Lemesurier)

Though Lemesurier's translations, which attempt to include the rhyming nature of Nostradamus's originals, differ somewhat from other translations, he, like others, can hardly be blamed for connecting this passage, so full of detail, with the death of Catherine de Medici's husband, then King of France. In 1559, decked out in a golden helmet, he met Conte de Montgomery, the captain of his guard, in a duel. Both men carried the shields of their respective lineage, both of which featured the lion, rampant, in their devices. Their first match was completely even, but during the second encounter, the younger Montgomery's lance shattered and two sections impaled the King. The first caught him in the throat. The second, longer splinter penetrated the King's eye, lodging in his brain and, eventually, after nearly two weeks of intense agony, killing him.

Did You Know? Before it was decided that *Millennium* was catchier, the show's working title was *2000*.

It's that sort of maybe-maybe not quality to the *Prophesies* that have kept people interested. Though the timeline is certainly questionable, a significant number of the quatrains do contain dates which have coincided rather neatly with the specific events of the quatrain. He apparently foresaw the beginning of the French Revolution and the end of the monarchy occuring in, yes, 1792.

The quatrain that directly concerns Millennialists is X-72:

>The year 1999, seventh month,
>From the sky will come a great King of Terror:
>To bring back to life the great King of the Mongols,
>Before and after Mars to reign by good luck.
>
>(Omerian translation)

TESTIMONY TRIVIA 1

Luckily, not all of us have Frank Black's unique view of the world. Most of us wouldn't want it. However, we'd all like to think we were semi-observant, that we'd perform slightly better than an Alzheimer's patient if we found ourselves compelled to testify about what we'd seen at a crime scene. But would we? Keep track of your score until the end. See if you'd be a candidate for the Millennium Group.

QUESTIONS

1. What was the name of the peep-show club where the Killer met his female victim?
2. How much was the Killer willing to pay for a mere ten-minute private viewing at the peep show?
3. How long had the Blacks been living in Washington, DC, before moving back to Washington state?
4. What reason does Frank Black give to his old friend, Lt Robert Bletcher, for moving back to Seattle?
5. In the course of the pilot episode, two of Frank's former cases are mentioned. Give yourself a point for the name of each of the two killers.
6. What did Frank Black find written on both a makeshift coffin and the underside of a bridge?
7. And what was written on the second coffin?
8. What two poets are quoted in this episode?
9. What does Frank bring Jordan as a sort of 'Get Well Soon' gift?
10. What arrived in the Blacks' mail at the end of the opening episode?

While the sense of the quatrain, that July 1999 is the date of some apocalyptic confrontation, has been generally agreed upon, the details are certainly up for debate – a debate that has widened with the attention of New Age 'scholars'. For example, the arrival of Martian meteorites has, in some minds, suggested that there may be a second meaning to the verse, one completely unrelated to Mars as the God of War, or Mars as a zodiacal sign, but perhaps related to contact with an extraterrestrial race, a theme popular among New Age practitioners. Others, however, wonder if Nostradamus, reputed, despite his interest in things esoteric, to be a fairly devout Catholic, wasn't already writing into the Christian millennialistic traditions or, in light of his investigation by French authorities, attempting to appear to follow that theological bent.

By the time Nostradamus died on 2 July, 1566, he'd already become famous. Catherine de Medici, Queen of France, frequently sought his insights and advice. Several times, his uncanny knack drew the attention of French magistrates who thought he was just too specific, too accurate to be a fraud. Their investigations became serious enough to send Nostradamus fleeing persecution in Paris. Yet, despite the many influences suspected of corrupting the expression of his prophecies, they have never been out of print in the four centuries since his death. History knows him as a physician, philosopher and poet. Time will tell whether he was also a prophet.

ANSWERS

1 The Ruby Tip
2 $200
3 Ten years
4 The weather
5 Leon Cole Pigitt and Ed Cuffle
6 'PESTE' – the Plague
7 La Grande Dame
8 William Butler Yeats and Nostradamus
9 A puppy
10 Polaroid photos

YOUR SCORE:

NOTE BOOK:

Taking over Friday nights

When Fox executives decided to shift *The X-Files* out of its wildly-successful Friday night slot, to make room for *Millennium*, many fans felt themselves the victim of overly-overt network manipulation. Even Chris Carter and *X-Files* star David Duchovny didn't seem sure how to respond.

'I like to think of *The X-Files* as being abducted!'

CHRIS CARTER

'You feel a little bit like … ya know … you were an only child for a while and then, all of a sudden, you've got a little brother and maybe you want to go to the crib at night – and drop a rock on its head.'

DAVID DUCHOVNY, *ENTERTAINMENT TONIGHT*

However, the move to Sunday started *The X-Files* on their highest rated season to date, and *Millennium* posting higher ratings than its 'big brother' did during its first season.

WHO'D BELIEVE SUCH EERIE IMAGES COULD LURK BEHIND THIS CHARMING GRIN?

INCIDENTALS:

Before fans start swarming over Seattle seeking the beautiful yellow house, or trying to send mail to Frank, they should know that the Blacks' address (1910 Ezekiel Drive, Seattle, WA, 98924) is fictional. The actual Yellow House is at Fourth and Fourth in New Westminster, British Columbia, Canada.

☐

GETTING READY FOR
THE PEEP SHOW
SCENES

'Getting into character' can be a scary experience when you work on a show like *Millennium*. When questioned after the show's big screen première, both leads confessed to having trouble sleeping. Megan Gallagher suffered through a nightmare; Lance Henriksen discovered how hard it was to shake off his compelling character when he found himself skulking through his home locking doors and windows in the middle of the night.

□

After his phenomenal success with *The X-Files*, Carter asked for – and got! – an almost unheard of budget for a television program. As he's proven since, however, he and his crew can do a whole heck of a lot with 1.5 *million* dollars per episode.

Comments to the press that he'd continue on with *The X-Files* if he was offered '*Seinfeld* money', however, didn't sit well with some fans.

CASE FILE: 'Gehenna'

CASE SYNOPSIS:

When a bunch of eager-beaver young salesmen turn up as fertilizer in a public rose garden, the Millennium Group turns its not inconsiderable resources to discovering why. The trail leads back to a marketing cult with a rather unique way of disposing of those salesmen who don't show any affinity for shampoo sales. On a much more personal level, Frank's glimpses into the Killer's mind leave him questioning his previous belief – that the 'beasts' stalking society are all human.

KEY CITATION:

'I've seen the face of evil, Frank.
I've looked into its eyes. Seen it staring
back at me. But, the face has always been
a man's face, a human's face. I've always
believed that evil is born in a cold heart
and a weak mind.'

MIKE ATKINS,
THE MILLENNIUM GROUP

VITAL STATISTICS:

Original US Airdate:	01/11/96
Production Number:	4C01
Written by:	Chris Carter
Directed by:	David Nutter

Guest Cast:

Terry O'Quinn	Peter Watts
Don Mackay	Jack Meredith
Chris Ellis	Jim Penseyres
Robin Gammell	Mike Atkins
Sam Kouth	Dylan
Stephen Holmes	Eedo Bolow
George Josef	Mr Bolow
Nina Persachi	Mrs Bolow
Henry Watson	The Detective
Chris Bradford	The Driver
Don McWilliams	The Park Guy

Death Toll:	2 Male Victims (1 immolated in microwave, 1 'scared to death') Unknown Number of Male Victims, immolated

CASE HISTORY:

MARKETING CULTS: THE NEW AGE RELIGION

It took the Millennium Group's Mike Atkins about two seconds to identify Eedo Bolow's real problem – cult control. Stripped of the special effects, the disjointed visions of an ex-FBI agent, and the looming presence of the Apocalypse, this could have been almost any episode of *Homicide* or *Law & Order*.

Mixing visions of The Beast with hard-ball telemarketing did more than just ensure the plot was a true *Millennium* episode. It also illuminated the range of activities now understood to be cultism. Up until 1986, the public perception of cults seemed limited to the saffron-robed 'monks' selling daisies in international airports. Sort of an extreme hippie, they were more nuisance than danger. Then came tales of 'Moonies' and their ilk. Teenagers, stripped of their financial support and community, were 'persuaded' to criminal acts or simply dumped, often half-starved and drugged, on the street when their usefulness was expended. With awareness came apprehension that something so destructive could have snared thousands without anyone really noticing! Public fear of cults probably reached its height in the late 1980s and early 1990s when so-called 'Satanic' cults became the hot talk-show topic and dozens of teachers, daycare workers and medical professionals were accused, unjustly, of 'black rituals' and vaguely 'occult practices' enacted against the weakest members of society.

However, the notion that 'cultism' could exist without obvious accessories like rough cotton robes, shaven heads or a blatantly charismatic leader didn't really occur to the general public until Amway, a massive, multi-level marketing machine, suddenly came under fire and the catchphrase 'marketing cult' was born.

That some businesses are strict hierarchies goes without saying, it certainly doesn't make them 'cults'. Likewise, the demarkation point between a cult and a mainstream religion is arguably a simple matter of numbers. Yet, marketing cults do indeed exist and by taking it to the extreme in 'Gehenna', the *Millennium* crew had little difficulty in illustrating the common links between all self-destructive cults, and creating an organization capable of blending shampoo and sarin gas. In fact, 'Gehenna' provides an almost perfect checklist of the factors that distinguish marketing cults from other typical, if high-powered, sales forces, and indeed, other religions.

DECEPTION. While it's easy to make an argument that all marketing involves a certain amount of deception, and that 'let the buyer beware' remains a necessary warning, marketing cults take it further. Like the fictional Gehenna International, marketing cults follow hidden agendas – often without the knowledge of their 'front' people. While Ricardo Clemmett's telemarketers would eventually realize he wanted to amass enough wealth and power to precipitate an Apocalypse, they weren't recruited with ads screaming 'Help Destroy the World!' Knowledge of Clemmett's real plans would come later as they were 'indoctrinated' higher in the hierarchy.

EXCLUSIVITY. Just like traditional cults, marketing cults prey on the least secure members of any group by offering them the *semblance* of something they want – usually inclusion. Marketing cults are usually quick to 'advance' their recruits, giving them the illusion of entrance into the 'upper workings' of the group. They encourage them to recruit others so they can have their own group to 'manage'. The reality is usually a set of meaningless 'ranks' that satisfy egos without ever handing over real power or important information.

ALIENATION. Giving those 'ranks' meaning is usually accomplished by several related techniques that, in combination, cut the recruit off from the real world. Physical separation is the first step. The 'Company' might push the recruit to share digs with other salespeople, where 'they can share marketing technique', 'form advantageous relationships within the Company', 'save valuable marketing time getting to work sooner', or simply 'enjoy the Company's many recreational facilities' and – in the process – surround the recruit with only those people who believe in the validity of the ranks and the Company!

Group dynamics can make reasonable people believe it's perfectly reasonable to put in several hours of intense exercise before work, hit the streets until late at night, socialize until the wee hours, and be back in that gym on less than four hours sleep. That sleep-deprived people are more likely to accept other forms of manipulation, or that there's no room for former friends or family in this artificially-hectic lifestyle, seldom occurs to the sleep-deprived person. Like Below, recruits are encouraged to see the Company as an extended family. Any derogatory statements by those outside the Company are, of course, based on 'envy, mis-information, or a lack of vision'.

UNDUE INFLUENCE. In 'Gehenna' it was drugs and screens of 'motivational' messages; in most cults, however, especially at an entry level, it's usually more subtle. For example, new recruits may be exposed to an apparently successful, well-dressed 'sales force' who all drive Beemers and constantly discuss their huge stock portfolios, all with the unspoken understanding that these people are representative of the entire sales team. In fact, they are usually recruiters who've never sold anything! The real sales force is outside, ringing doorbells from eight in the morning to ten or

LANCE HENRIKSEN'S FACE SEEMS INCAPABLE OF BEING BADLY LIT

eleven at night. They don't drive Beemers, they don't have stock portfolios, they probably don't have more than one good work suit. They all share one belief, however, that the reason they're still banging on doors is that they haven't come up to the same mark everyone else already has.

EXPLOITATION. Needless to say, no one expends that much energy on anything without a reasonable expectation of realizing some return on their investment. With marketing cults, the expected return on investment is always financial. The fictional Eedo Bolow claimed he 'burned' all his previous possessions and, while that big microwave certainly makes it a possibility, similar phraseology has also been used symbolically by captured marketing cultists who, in reality, simply gave over their possessions to their new 'family'. In most cases, the possessions find their way to the marketplace and the cash is pocketed by the cult. Though Bolow was probably broke when he was recruited, and his personal wealth wasn't going to do much to help

Gehenna International's coffers, as virtual slave labor, he was invaluable – as long as he continued to sell. Though most cults don't nuke their less productive employees, they are often left, penniless, without the support network of their erstwhile 'friends' who are encouraged to shun slackers who'd only 'pull them down', and without family contacts as a result of the isolation imposed by the Company.

In the episode 'Gehenna', the *Millennium* crew took the intrinsic misery that only humans seem capable of inflicting on one another, took it to the extremes illustrated by Tokyo's real-life terrorists, and added the supernatural element that all too many of us are willing to believe must be responsible for such horrors. People couldn't do this, could they?

NOTEBOOK:

Tracking 'Gehenna' To Its Roots

If you were confused by the apparent conflict between Frank's dictionary reference, which claimed 'gehenna' was a New Testament term, and Mike Atkins' assertion that the term was archaic and found in the Old Testament, you weren't alone. In fact, both were correct – just incomplete. 'Gehenna', actually the 'Greek-acized' version of the Old Hebrew for 'hell', appears several times throughout both the Old and New Testaments. Regardless of chapter or verse, however, it's not the sort of place for vacations!

Early references in the Old Testament actually gave an exact location for Gehenna, a ravine in the lands of Hinnom, just south of Jerusalem. Sometime between Hinnom's time and the turn of the first millennium, tenth century Judaism turned this admitted inhospitable place into the site where the generally dreaded Last Judgement was to take place. Oddly, in both Joshua (15:8, 18:16) and Nehemiah (11:30), Gehenna is portrayed almost as a refuge. In Joshua, the Jews coming out of the wilderness actually *fought* for it! In

Nehemiah, no one was fighting for it, but they huddled down there for some time after exile in Babylonia.

Later references, however, abandoned any illusion that Gehenna was less than a Hell on earth. In 2 Chronicles (28:3), Ahaz, a king of highly questionable morals and a despotic rule, forced his own children to walk through Gehenna, a place of burning, to satisfy the God Molech. Apparently, he wasn't the only one practicing that custom. In 2 Kings, Josiah, a king of an entirely different temperament, tore down and destroyed the Gehennian altars to prevent parents from burning their children alive. Jeremiah (7:32) promises that God will punish Israel for the sacrifice of its children, that Gehenna will be called the 'Valley of Slaughter' for the number of Israelites God will allow to fall to their enemies.

FRANK'S MENTOR, MIKE ATKINS (ROBIN GAMMELL), SHOULD HAVE REMEMBERED WHAT HANSEL AND GRETEL DID TO THE WITCH!

In the New Testament, however, 'Gehenna' no longer refers to a specific place. Throughout Matthew and Mark, Gehenna is synonymous with more modern interpretations of Hell. Gehenna, in Matthew (5:22), is called the 'place of fire'. In James, 'tongues' of fire consume the entire world. The millennial concept of cycles of death and rebirth, of building and destruction, is tied directly to the 'fires of Gehenna', the fires of Hell.

So, from a valley depicted in a general accounting of land ownership, to the site of 'evil' temples, to the literal place of the Apocalypse, to an abstract Hell ready to consume the soul instead of the body, 'Gehenna' is a term found throughout both Testaments. Perhaps, if the prophets had been writing in the age of industrial-scale microwaves, the nasty King Ahaz would have been 'nuking' his children instead of tossing them on the fire.

Measuring Our Future By Inches: The Great Pyramid at Giza

The Great Pyramid of Giza looms large, both figuratively and literally, in human history but, surprisingly, despite decades of intense research, we know relatively little about it. Is it four thousand years old? Or nine thousand? We don't know. Why was it built? We don't know. For whom was it built? We don't know.

We do, however, know exactly how big it is, inside and out, down to mere fractions of an inch and it's in those numbers that two men, John and Morton Edgar, found a correlation that only increases the mystery of this already mysterious edifice.

After measuring hallways and chambers, walls and angles, they assigned a new value to the simple inch. They let it equal 365.242, the exact number of days in the solar year. With this as their yardstick, they began the creation of an architectural timeline. The length of one room, multiplied by the solar year, fell neatly on the birth of Christ. From there to the Hall of Truth in Light, their next measurement pinpointed 7 April, 30 (CE), the generally agreed date of Christ's crucifixion. Other measurements, when applied to our modern calendar, landed squarely on the start of World War I in 1914 and the exact date of the outbreak of World War II. Astronomical events like the devastation of Tunguska, Siberia, by some catastrophic impact and significant geological events, the Krakatowa eruption for one, are also found in the meticulous measurements.

Using established events as their guideline, investigators have also pinpointed a number of 'unknowns', future dates taken from measurements, points on the timeline, that have yet to occur. Like almost every other form of prophesy known to the West, the 'Pyramid Prophets' have apparently taken special interest in the year 2000. Six different measurements are virtually identical, and all point to an Event occurring on 5 May, 2000.

TESTIMONY TRIVIA 2

QUESTIONS

1   What drug did Eedo's 'friends' give him?
2   Who wrote 'I smell blood and an era of prominent madmen'?
3   What was Frank installing in his house when he was called to San Francisco by the Millennium Group?
4   What did Jordan eventually name her dog?
5   What, other than ashes, did someone find in the rose gardens of a San Francisco park?
6   How many adult humans did Jim Penseyers suggest could account for 39 pounds of carbonized remains?
7   What do Frank Black and Peter Watts find in the burned out dry-cleaners?
8   How long has Frank Black been receiving anonymous photographs of his family?
9   Take a point for each of the projected 'slogans' you recall seeing in the telemarketing center.
10 What name do all the telemarketers use?
11 Where did Eedo Bolow once attend school?
12 To whom does Catherine compare Frank?
13 What unusual item does the Killer wear?
14 What frightening substance, linked to the Tokyo subway attacks, was found on the second victim?
15 What was the Killer's name?

What sort of incident? Well, considering the catastrophic nature of the other events supposedly predicted in the pyramid, and the fact that even the date of the Krakatowa explosion, felt around the world, was only recorded once, believers are awaiting something very similar in magnitude to the Armageddon forecast by Christian literalists. That May 5, 2000 will be the date of a particularly strong planetary alignment does little to ease New Age fears.

However, as explained by Mike Atkins in 'Gehenna', there's some disagreement over the measurements and their resultant predictions. If, as some geologists and astronomers believe, the solar year has changed somewhat in the past four

A NSWERS

1 LSD
2 W H Auden
3 A security light
4 Benny
5 The remains of a human ear
6 About seven
7 A set of human teeth
8 Three years
9 'CREATE DESIRE', 'EVERYONE
   WANTS BEAUTIFUL HAIR',
   'FACILITATE ENVY', and
   'WORK WILL SET YOU FREE'
10 Bob Smith
11 Petaluma Community College
12 The Catcher in the Rye
13 Night-vision goggles
14 Sarin
15 Ricardo Clemmett

YOUR SCORE:

to nine thousand years, then the calculations need some adjustment. The results, however, aren't at all comforting, merely moving the date of the Apocalypse earlier, to 1998.

INCIDENTALS:

Eschatology: The theological or academic study of the Second Coming, Final Judgement and the Apocalypse.

☐

ACTOR FILMOGRAPHY:
DON MACKAY

Whether you've pegged Jack Meredith, the Blacks' neighbor, as the Polaroid Stalker, a Millennium Group watchdog, or just the nosiest TV neighbour since Mrs Kravitz peered through Samantha's window on *Bewitched*, he certainly adds a lighter touch to the overwhelming gloom of the *Millennium* universe.

The Halfback of Notre Dame (1996) – Father O'Malley
The Man Who Wouldn't Die (1995) – Henry Graham
Beyond Obsession (1994) – Judge Mahoney
Hands of a Stranger (1987) – Judge Forester
Body of Evidence (1988) – Justice of the Peace

He's also, of course, an *X-Files* alumnus!

CASE FILE: 'Dead Letters'

CASE SYNOPSIS:

Frank's investigation of a sadistic serial killer is hampered when James Horn, a prospective new member of the Millennium Group becomes emotionally involved with the case. In addition to the normal strain such a case brings, James seems determined to 'out profile' the formidable Frank Black. When that fails, James inserts himself deeper into the investigation, and into dangers that even Frank couldn't have foreseen.

KEY CITATION:

'Frank, I'm going to be right upfront about this. I've heard a lot about you, a lot, and don't get me wrong, I have the utmost respect for your work, but, I gotta tell ya … I'm doubtful about some of the things I've heard about you.'

JAMES HORN

VITAL STATISTICS:

Original US Airdate:	11/08/96
Production Number:	4C02
Written by:	Glen Morgan and James Wong
Directed by:	Thomas J Wright

Guest Cast:

Chris Ellis	Jim Penseyres
Ron Halder	The Killer
James Morrison	Jim Horn
Garvin Cross	The Patient
Anthony Harrison	Detective Jenkins
Lisa R Vultaggio	Janice Sterling
Rob Morton	Lewis
Maria Louisa Figura	Cindy Horn
Cooper Olsen	TC Horn
Michelle Hart	Marjorie Holden
Fulvio Cecere	The Security Guard
Andrew Laurenson	The Clown
Allison Warren	Officer Sarah Stevens
Ken Shimizu	C.S.T. Member

Death Toll:	3 female, suffocated and dismembered

CASE HISTORY:

THE RETURN TO THE SCENE OF THE CRIME On any

other program, a crime scene stakeout, two cops sitting around in a car while nothing much happens, would be just the sort of lull in the action that sends viewers to the fridge. Not so in *Millennium*, not when Frank Black's stakeout is a cleverly staged lure, and not when the scene is packed with the sort of real world detail that comes from careful research into the nature of killers.

When characters mimic real agents, becoming proactive strategists instead of flat-footed bumblers waiting for the criminal to prove himself an even greater bumbler, viewers invest the scene with their own curiosity and expectations – and stay glued to the set. Black isn't just a spectacular observer – he's a player playing the same tension-filled game that profilers have enacted across the United States.

Among the many scenarios available to the *Millennium* crew were the tragic events played out in the Atlanta Child Murder Cases. Faced with a killer who'd proven himself a fanatic follower of his own press, the FBI's Behavioral Sciences unit suggested a staged event very much like the one later played out in 'Dead Letters'. Atlantan law enforcement personnel identified crime scenes, locales where the bodies were later dumped, and a neighborhood church as sites likely to evoke strong emotional responses in the killer and erected a series of 'memorial' crosses. While the one destined for the church was larger, white crosses less than a foot high dotted roadsides and other, more remote, spots around the city.

BLOOPER! The 'special effect' which changed the tweezers picked up by the Killer into a writing implement for his minuscule messages was completely unintentional!

Why were they so small? Quite simply, to encourage theft. A significant percentage of criminals claim mementos, 'trophies', from their victims as part of the original attack, but, as the Atlanta Child Murderer had already expounded at some length on his belief that the police were idiots, those same officers were hoping the crosses would prove irresistible, another way for the killer to rub their noses in his success. Even if the killer didn't actually attempt to take one of the crosses, undercover personnel could record those individuals who came to the sites, note the license numbers of motorists slowing to look at them, and perhaps discover a 'pilgrim', someone who felt compelled to visit all the locations. While curiosity might cause the casual passer-by to slow or stop for a moment, even leave flowers, 'casual' mourners wouldn't seek out every site. For the killer, such a trek could prove euphoric.

In 'Dead Letters', the even smaller crosses left at the nurse's memorial provided a cinematographic equivalent (but more easily filmed) lure for its egotistic fictional killer.

FRANK AND JAMES
HORN (PLAYED BY
JAMES MORRISON)
EYE THE SETTING
THEY HOPE WILL
LURE OUT A KILLER

Such public 'stages', events enacted to goad a killer into the open, are frequently accompanied by sympathetic reporting. When a koala bear, one of many collected by a young female victim of another serial killer, was left at her graveside in South Carolina, pictures of the potential trophy made the front pages of several statewide papers. For the typically narcissistic killer who avidly searches the headlines for some mention of his latest 'art', the photo served as an engraved invitation to appear at a location chosen by law enforcement.

Amazingly enough, the invitation is usually accepted. Though often taken as cliché, the fact remains that criminals often do return to the scene of the crime. Whether to maintain some 'contact' with the deceased, or the investigation, or to relive the experience in fantasy, killers have been known to roll in the dirt where a kill was made, to dump corpses within feet of one another, and drag subsequent victims to the site of their first kill before disposing of them.

One killer, Martin Beesbrook, spent twelve years in jail for murdering Constance Baker. On being released, he promptly bought the vacant lot where he'd killed and mutilated her almost beyond recognition and built his bungalow over it before erecting a white picket fence around the property. Why? So he could sleep above the spot where she'd died.

Given this seemingly undeniable urge, staking out crime scenes and victim graves has become increasingly common and, with the advent of high quality surveillance equipment, more sophisticated. Unfortunately, as happened in 'Dead Letters', any stakeout, even one as carefully orchestrated as the fictional one set up by Frank Black, can go wrong.

A case in point is that of Mary Kellerman. After being told by FBI profilers that they could expect the killer to sneak into the cemetery, police diligently staked out her grave. Sure enough, in the middle of the night, with no mourners to witness anything, a man crept into the graveyard. His sobbing voice, begging for forgiveness, claiming it had all been an accident, echoed to the officers concealed nearby. Needless to say, they quickly sprang their trap – only to realize the grave the man was huddled over was the one *next* to their victim. The man turned out to be the hit and run driver who'd killed the woman some time previous to the crime currently being investigated. The police had solved a crime, just the wrong one. Press coverage of the night's activities made a second attempt blatantly impractical.

Even skilled surveillance teams can be spotted – and circumvented. When agents staked out the apartment of Chicago killer Jack Raymond, Raymond simply set fire to a vacant apartment on the floor below, waited for the police to respond to a neighbor's panicked shouts, then waltzed into his apartment, retrieved damning evidence from inside, and disappeared.

The fictional scenario enacted in 'Dead Letters', taken straight from the pages of FBI operations, did considerably more than provide Frank and his partner the opportunity to pour out their marital troubles to one another. Like the inclusion of an orange VW van, which an FBI profiler once identified as the vehicle of choice for serial killers, the details packed into the stakeout scene gave audiences a window into the proven strategies real-life investigators employ.

NOTEBOOK:

Of Snakes and Circles

The circle, the ring, the 'snake eating itself', that arcane symbol featured in the opening credits and since taken as *Millennium*'s symbol, is yet another borrowing from a number of mythologies. In Norway, it's the great serpent that encircles Midgard, our earth. Like the story recounted in *The X-Files* episode 'Dod Kalm', it's part of both the creation and apocalypse stories of Scandinavia. The serpent coils about the world, holding everything together until Ragnarok, the Norse Armageddon. Its symbolism, that of eternity's end, and the downfall of order, are particularly appropriate in a series concerned with the end of the world and humanity's descent into chaos.

In Old Britain, before the advent of Christianity, the simplified emblem, an unbroken Circle, also symbolized the turning of a life, or of time itself, the beginning and the end all contained in one image.

For Christians, the snake, symbol of the Devil's Temptation of Eden, is tied to both man's first fall from grace and the 'Antichrist' of the coming Apocalypse. Yet, despite the weighty and chaotic imagery associated with it, the Uroborus is almost universally considered a symbol of *hope*.

The Circle, in simple or animalistic form, is never a true ending. Rather, it represents the closing of a cycle which, by its very nature, also implies a series of endless beginnings, a continuous rejuvenation. For the most optimistic, the Circle depicts an eternal chance to begin again – to get it right.

TESTIMONY TRIVIA 3

Most of us will never see crime scenes the way Frank Black does – which may be a blessing – but, did you catch the more ordinary details? See how you stack up against the average eye-witness.

1 What number appears on Frank's pager when the Millennium Group contacts him?
2 What was used to cover the victims' faces?
3 Which coffee shop does Frank frequent in Seattle?
4 Who was the subject of James Horn's most notable case?
5 What piece of evidence did Frank expect to find near the body of the first victim?
6 What odd construct is a talk-show host seen wearing in this episode?
7 How does James Horn like his burgers?
8 What does the killer write his messages on?
9 What word did the killer add to his cross?
10 What was the murdered nurse's first name?
11 How many pins were handed out for the memorial?
12 What was the hotline number of the suspect flyer?
13 What was the name of the 1-hr optician the Killer frequented?
14 What ruse did James Horn use to arrange a confrontation with the Killer?
15 What change did James Horn make in his appearance after assaulting the Killer?

INCIDENTALS:

TC, the fictional son of James Horn, was named after James Morrison's previous character on *Space: Above and Beyond*, Col TC McQueen.

☐

Just as the *Millennium* crew draw many of the details for their fictional killers, like the reference for orange VW vans, from accounts of real-world agents and cases, Lance Henriksen, a superb character actor, bases much of his performance on readings by John Douglas, the ex-FBI agent who inspired

ANSWERS

1   2000
2   Duct tape
3   Molly's Coffee Shop
4   The 'Highway 8' Killer
5   A written message
6   An 'empathy belly'
7   Medium.
8   Gray hairs
9   'VENTURED'
10 Marjorie
11 30
12 1-503-555-0505
13 Spectacles
14 A flat tire
15 He shaved off his moustache
    and beard

YOUR SCORE:

Silence of the Lambs and wrote *Mindhunter*. It's a character he sometimes has difficulty shaking off at the end of the day.

□

One of the many realities facing would-be television production crews is the ever-present Censor Board. These shadowy figures decide whether or not the viewing public is ready for the artist's 'creation'. In addition to decisions based on sexual and violent content, the Board also judges the 'tastefulness' of a given presentation. Getting any mention of 'defecation', covered or not, past them could have been a major headache in itself, but *Millennium*'s representative gives them just enough latitude to work their magic.

□

Brittany Tiplady, who plays the young Jordan Black, was so scared by the clown scene that she was afraid to go to bed that night.

□

Clowning Around: Several famous serial killers have a connection to clowns – most infamous of them all is John Wayne Gacy who, at his trial, cited his entertaining at children's parties while decked out as a clown as evidence of his pillar-of-the-community status. It's more likely he was indulging a less active aspect of his raging pedophilia. In this episode, however, the reference is actually to a nightmare that one of the writers still vividly remembers from his own childhood.

ANDREW LAURENSON PLAYS A TERRIFYING CLOWN

▶ ▶ ▶ ▶ ▶ ▶

THE PROFILER'S PRIMER:

A GLOSSARY OF CRIME SCENE AND LAW ENFORCEMENT TERMINOLOGY

AUTOEROTICISM: Sexual arousal and/or sexual gratification without a partner. In 'Dead Letters', Raymond Dees substitutes explosions for dates.

BLITZ: A guerilla-style attack where the assailant strikes with such initial force or surprise that the victim has no chance of retaliating. The original attack is often from behind or, as happened when Eedo Bolow was herded into the dry-cleaning warehouse in 'Gehenna', from above.

DEFENSIVE WOUNDS: Usually found on the fingers, hands and forearms, these injuries result from a victim's attempts to ward off an attacker. The absence of such wounds may indicate the victim knew the attacker, or be indicative of a blitz attack.

DEPERSONALIZATION: Attempts by the attacker to objectify or generalize the victim. Such actions may include physically destroying the victim's face, covering the face with a pillow, sheet, or item of clothing, or, as in 'Dead Letters', with duct tape. It may also be as simple as turning the victim face down. These actions may take place during the crime, but often occur post-mortem as well.

OVERKILL: Excessive force used in the commission of a murder. The killer doesn't just kill, but physically assails the victim. In 'Blood Relatives', Mrs Cort isn't just murdered, she's stabbed multiple times over her entire body. Often taken as an indication of extreme rage.

PERSONATION: Closely related to staging, personation is almost anything a criminal does at the crime scene other than commit the crime. For example, in 'The Wild and The Innocent', Billy Webber kills the elderly Nesbitts and then walks away. In 'Dead Letters', the killer engages in a whole series of actions that have meaning for him, a ritual that accompanies each killing. Personation can include posing the body, mutilating it in some way, leaving some symbolic item at a crime scene, or reciting a series of words over the body. It differs from staging in that the acts are of significance to the criminal, and are not necessarily intended to leave a message for investigators.

PSYCHOLOGICAL AUTOPSY: An investigation into the deceased person's life. Usually undertaken by a psychiatrist or psychologist, it's an attempt to discover what, if any, psychological factors might have been involved in the person's death.

SIGNATURE: A serial offender's ritualistic behaviors. Usually linked to staging and personation, this behavior is often distinctive enough to allow investigators to identify a perpetrator involved in different types of crime.

SOUVENIRS: Anything taken away by the offender as a 'memento' of the event. Frequently taken items include jewelery, clothing, anything with the victim's name or picture, anything personal. Some investigators make a distinction between souvenirs and 'trophies', defining a trophy as a part of the victim's body such as hair, skin, organs, fingernails. The nurse's nametag in 'Dead Letters' would be a typical souvenir.

STAGING: A deliberate attempt to change the crime scene from its original state. Criminals do it to throw off suspicion. For example, ransacking a residence after a murder to make the scene appear to be an interrupted burglary instead of a contract hit. Other individuals may change the scene to protect the sensibilities of the family, covering a naked body to protect the deceased's modesty for example. A common criminal staging is to burn a crime scene or to attempt to burn a victim.

UNDOING: An act of remorse by the offender, usually in the form of removing the *appearance* of a crime. Washing a rape victim's body is a fairly classic example. So is wrapping a child's dead body in a blanket before disposing of it. If the killer feels no remorse, he'll likely just dump the body. Indications of hatred or disdain might include posing the body in a way certain to dismay the family and whoever finds it. Undoing attempts to lessen the impact of an existing crime.

VICTIMOLOGY: Similar to a criminal case history which attempts to build as complete as possible a picture of the criminal, a victimology is a complete description of the victims. It will usually include a personal history, with as many details as possible, employment history, educational history, and statements from numerous family members, friends and acquaintances. The hope is that, by comparing victimologies, investigators can find out *why* this particular individual became a victim.

CASE FILE: 'The Judge'

CASE SYNOPSIS:

When a vigilante extremist with illusions of grandeur starts sending out body parts by priority post, Frank Black, the Seattle Police Department and even the Millennium Group are hard pressed to explain how three murders, clearly connected by both method and intent, could have been committed by at least two different men! Even Frank's stoic faith in the system is shaken when the law seems incapable of prosecuting the real killer, a man who Frank freely admits never laid a hand on the victims.

CHRIS ELLIS AND CCH POUNDER ADD DEPTH TO THE CASTING OF THE MILLENNIUM GROUP

KEY CITATION:

'Mine is not a court of law, Mr Bardale. It is a
court of justice. We cannot address every
case. Our scope is not broad, like the
common-law courts. It is narrower, deeper,
more pure. Our judgement, final.'

THE JUDGE

VITAL STATISTICS:

Original US Airdate: 15/11/96

Production Number: 4C04
    Written by: Ted Mann
    Directed by: Randy Zisk

Guest Cast:
Marshall Bell	The Judge
Chris Ellis	Jim Pensyres
CCH Pounder	Cheryl Andrews
Stephen James Lang	Detective Teeple
Michael Puttonen	Pathologist Massey
David Fredericks	Jonathan Mellen
Kirsten Williamson	Mail Room Worker
John Hawkes	Mr Bardale
J R Bourne	Carl Nearman
Donna White	Annie Tisman
Eva DeViveiros	Assistant DA Aquila
Kate Robbins	Marilyn
Beverly Elliot	Terry
Gabe Khouth	Parcel Service Employee

Death Toll: 2 males, bled to death after
involuntary amputation.
3 males known to have died off-
screen in previous incidents.
Total, unknown.

CASE HISTORY:

VIGILANTE JUSTICE: THE SELF-APPOINTED JUDGES

When *Millennium*'s 'Judge' hauled out his hood and passed judgement on his neighbors, he was simply harking back to that long-standing American tradition: vigilante justice. Whether as groups, or incredibly dedicated one-person courts, a disturbingly fast-growing section of the American populace, apparently disenchanted with the formal legal system, have elected themselves as officers of 'common law courts'. While frontier justice remained a common – and necessary – part of life in communities that might see a judge only once or twice a year, it was supposed to end with the availability of sitting courts at the last turn of the century. Instead, at the turn of this century, it's being revived in response to a judicial system that many feel is no longer 'of the People'.

In 1984, sixteen-year-old Melinda Wade, a bouncy high-school junior, was raped, mutilated and murdered. The entire process took nearly three days. Three days of horror that her father relived in nightmare after nightmare for the entirety of Mitchell Freid's six-year sentence – until Mitchell Freid was paroled for good behavior. The day Mitchell Freid was released, Harold Wade waited for him down the road from the state penitentiary and calmly shot him three times. Harold Wade received seventeen years for his crime, nearly three times the penalty levied against his daughter's murderer. The community protest was long, vocal, and made absolutely no difference at all.

It wasn't that the community wasn't capable of understanding the reasons for the differing sentences. Freid's lawyers argued successfully that, though Melinda was held for three days, her death wasn't premeditated. Freid showed considerable remorse during the trial and the penalty phase. He was already receiving counselling at the time of his trial and, according to his counsellor, was benefitting from the program. Harold Wade, on the other hand, spent years planning Freid's murder. He showed no remorse. At the penalty phase, he quietly, but firmly, declared, 'Your Honour, I swore to tell you the truth. As God is my witness, if I had it to do over again, I'd do it just the same.'

Intellectually, the sentences reflected a set of legal realities meant to address the 'rehabilitation' side of the judicial system.

Emotionally, the community remained angry and confused. For killing a child, an innocent with her whole life ahead of her, Freid was released after six years. For killing Freid, a convicted murderer, Harold Wade, after already losing his daughter, had now lost his own freedom. The law had been served in both cases, but a restless feeling remained with the community as a whole, the sneaking suspicion that 'justice' got lost in the shuffle.

One case like Harold Wade's might arouse public ire, the type of anger that finds expression in letters to the editor, in calls to congressmen, and some placard-waving in front of courtrooms. When already dissatisfied citizens discover similar 'miscarriages of justice' throughout their morning papers, 'alternative' justice systems begin receiving some serious consideration. In North America, a number of Native communities opted out of the federal legal system, called for self-government, and instigated Community Courts to hand out their own brand of justice. In some instances, 'common courts' enrich the lives of the communities they serve. The Navajo judicial system is often cited as a sparkling example of a community-based law enforcement and judicial system.

More often, however, alternative justice doesn't arise peaceably within the framework of existing codes. In the vast majority of cases, small groups, even individuals, simply decide, as Harold Wade did, to take justice into their own hands. And not all causes are as emotionally acceptable as Wade's.

Take Joseph Paul Franklin, for example. He firmly believed in the supreme Aryan positions put forward by Adolf Hitler. He saw blacks as 'factors undermining the fabric of American society'. According to Franklin, they 'formented dissent' by pushing for rights they 'were never meant to have'. When the government showed no sign of 'rectifying' this sad state of affairs, Franklin joined a string of 'alternative' political parties including the Klan, the American Nazi Party, and the National States Rights Party. Then he decided to take the matter personally in hand.

First, he shot Alphonse Manning and Toni Schwenn in Wisconsin. He was black, she was white, a situation Franklin found particularly disgusting. Franklin then went on to kill Harold McGiver in Georgia and Raymond Taylor across the country in Virginia just because they were black before striking at yet another inter-racial couple, Jesse Taylor and Marian Besette. Once again, he was black, she was white. The killing continued unabated. Lawrence Reese. Leo Watkins. Vernon Jordan (black and president of the National Urban League) was shot in Fort Wayne, Indiana, yet, miraculously, survived. Not so thirteen-year-old Dante Brown or his fourteen-year-old friend, Darrell Lane whom Franklin shot down in Cincinnati, Ohio. Then it was back to couple-killing, this time Kathleen Mikula and Arthur Smothers in Johnstown, Ohio. The killings continued. Eighteen-year-old David Martin and co-worker Ted Fields were gunned down in an intersection while jogging. His justification: he was 'cleaning up America'. Like so many 'mission killers', he made no real attempt to deny his guilt in any of the murders, though he continuously denied the attempt on Vernon Jordan. Most experts suspect that the reason for the denial has little to do with motive. They believe Franklin remains adamant to avoid being connected with a failure to complete his mission.

BLOOPER! Evidently The Judge didn't study his bible nearly as well as he thought he did. Just before he offers Frank a job working for him, he calls himself 'Legion' and relates a story of Jesus casting demons of the same name *out* of a herd of enchanted hogs. Unfortunately, according to both Mark (5:1-13) and Luke (8:28-34), Christ was actually casting the demons out of a man and *into* the pigs!

For Carroll Cole, 'loose women' were the bane of American existence and, sometime early in the 1970s, he took it upon himself to rid his homeland of these deplorable citizens. If all his post-arrest claims are to be believed, he was incredibly successful. According to Cole, he killed 35 to 40 'loose women' between 1971 and his 1981 trial on three murder charges. Cole admitted to his crimes almost immediately, and was sorry he couldn't prove all the murders he claimed, citing the fact that he was 'a drunken pisshead' most of that decade for his failure to recall all the details.

In Great Britain, another 'evangelical' killer was picked up just as Cole was preparing for his trial. Like his overseas contemporary, Peter Sutcliffe, the Yorkshire Ripper, was ridding England of as many 'prostitutes' as he could get his bloody hands on. He is known to have killed thirteen women in five years, battered, stabbed and mutilated more, and, apparently, felt absolutely no remorse for any of his actions. He claims to have embarked on this mission while working in a graveyard where he heard the voice of God emanating from the ground, telling him to kill these women. Considering the lack of religious background in Sutcliffe's makeup, however, along with the lack of staging that normally accompanies such killings, it's much more likely that Peter Sutcliffe was being entirely honest when he told his younger brother, 'I was just cleaning up streets, our kid. Just cleaning up streets.'

Vigilantism is an uncomfortable issue for most conscientious people. Put in Harold Wade's shoes, many a parent might be tempted to do exactly as he did. It's hard for us to dredge up sympathy for Wade's victim, a cold-blooded murderer. Yet, Freid's circumstances were, in one sense, no different from Emily Jackson's, killed by Peter Sutcliffe in 1976, or Kathlyn Blum's, whose life was strangled away by Carroll Cole in a dark San Francisco parking lot. All are equally dead. All lost their lives at the hands of an individual with no right or authority to deprive them of their futures.

In 'The Judge', the *Millennium* crew produced a suave killer who spent his off-hours farming, rehabilitating chronic criminals, and ridding the countryside of those crooks who'd somehow managed to beat the system, who got away with crimes the 'common' man could understand and appreciate.

CATCH IT? Although Frank didn't move his family back to Seattle until the summer of 1996, the white board behind the Pathologist studying the severed foot reminds staff to change their filters on 6 November, 1995! Either those filters are badly clogged by now or the set crew blooped on the dates. Likewise, one of the documents relating to Mr Tisman's appeal seemed to indicate he'd be appearing in court on 17 March, 1995. Highly unlikely as he would have been dead for at least three years!

While hardly a sympathetic character, The Judge was one many frustrated Americans could certainly comprehend, one that many might even applaud.

Vigilantism has been described by some as 'a reclamation, by the People, of the power they'd entrusted to a legal system that's proven itself flawed and unworthy of their faith'. Others point to cases like 'The Axeman of New Orleans' as an example of just how well the 'People' manage their own justice. That series of events began in 1911. That year, three Italian grocers and their spouses were slaughtered in their own beds by an axeman who chiseled out a piece of their back doors to gain access. Then there was a lull many attribute to the inconvenient intervention of World War I. In any case, by the spring of 1918, when everything was supposedly returning to normal, the Axeman struck again. Like the Rosettis, the Crustis, and the Schiambras, the 1918 victims, the Maggios, were killed in their bed after their assailant crept into the house through a broken back door and attacked them with an axe. For whatever reason, someone had taken a deep dislike to Italian grocers in the Big Easy – and he seemed unlikely to stop killing. Just one month later, another Italian couple were attacked in the small apartment behind and above their grocery store. The husband survived, the wife did not. Next hit was Joseph Romano. Though his nieces heard suspicious noises and alerted the police, the man escaped and Joseph Romano died in hospital a few days later.

Tension in the Italian community in New Orleans reached fever pitch. Citizens began arming themselves. When Tony Adamonti brought his date home late and tried to sneak her in the back door, he was almost decapitated by her nervous father, an Italian grocer. Soon, anyone caught in the alleyways behind the bustling shops came under suspicion. Several incident reports describe neighbors attacking one another, each believing they'd stumbled on the Axeman in the dark. Yet, at the height of this fear frenzy, the Axeman stopped. Months passed and nothing happened.

Then, in the spring of 1919, he struck with a vengeance. This time it was the Cortimiglia family who were targeted. Both Charles and Rosie would, miraculously, survive the savage battery that left Charles with a half-dozen deep

TESTIMONY TRIVIA 4

QUESTIONS

1   Name the bowling alley where the Killer tracked down his last victim and stole his tongue.
2   Where did The Judge find Mr Bardale?
3   Name the dog who found one of the victims in a leaf heap.
4   What was The Judge's preferred drink?
5   What did a startled postal worker see inside a package passing her X-ray machine?
6   What sort of seeds were found on the second victim's sock?
7   Bardale had a number tattooed on his neck. What?
8   What was The Judge's 'day job'?
9   What did The Judge call Frank Black?
10 Where did Frank and the police find The Judge's body?

wounds and Rosie with a broken skull. Their infant daughter, however, died of the one blow leveled at her.

Two men were eventually arrested for the murders, but, as the killings continued, it quickly became evident that the wrong men were in jail. In the late summer of the same year, grocer Steve Boca's head was cracked open, but, he too survived! Unfortunately, as often happens after head injuries, he could give police nothing further to work with.

Nearly three months later, Mike Pepitone's wife awoke to hear wild scufflings in an adjoining room. Rushing in, she saw a man flee through an open window and her husband, dead, lying in the midst of their blood-soaked bed.

For whatever reason, The Axeman of New Orleans suddenly stopped knocking on his neighbors' doors and killing them. The Pepitones would be his last target in New Orleans.

Over a year later, in December of 1920, a woman 'heavily veiled' in black, stepped onto a Los Angeles street, raised a pistol, and emptied it into the body of Joseph Mumfre. She didn't attempt to escape, didn't struggle when police took her into custody. Eventually, she calmly explained that she was Mrs Michael Pepitone of New Orleans, that Joseph

Mumfre of Los Angeles was, until about a year ago, also a resident of New Orleans, and that he was the man who had hacked her husband to death.

Why Mrs Pepitone decided to become Mumfre's judge and executioner remains something of a mystery considering the active investigation of the New Orleans police. Though asked several times, there's no apparent record of her reasoning. With Mumfre dead, there's also no explanation for why he'd taken such a dislike to Italian grocers. What is undeniable, however, is that The Axeman of New Orleans never claimed another victim, and that Mrs Mike Pepitone served only three of her ten-year sentence.

NOTEBOOK:

And When *Does* the Millennium Start ... Really?

That's harder to determine than you might think. Flipping through your Day-Planner it seems sort of obvious, 1 January, 2000, right? The day after thousands of computers realize their programmers weren't too far-sighted, that they didn't plan beyond 1999, that all those computer-generated calendars now read *1900*! Computer glitches aside though, there was no year 0000, which means we'll have to wait until 1 January, 2001 to account for our full allotment of 2000 years of Christendom. There is precedent. The Vatican didn't believe that we had entered the 20th century until 1 January, 1901.

Of course, historically speaking, neither 2000 nor 2001 is likely to be accurate. If, as many theologians and historians believe, Christ was born about 4 BC, we'll be waiting for the magical two thousand years until 2005! Add in the fact that, well, no one really kept track of time in the Gregorian sense until an entire millennium had already passed, making dates somewhat speculative at the best, and the question of which thousand, or two thousand, years we're discussing rather murky. And then there's the Julian to Gregorian switchover ...

It seems there are only two certainties we can attribute to the year 2000. One, the New Year's party that year is going to put all others to shame. One travel firm is already sold out on packages to take their clients to the International Date Line so they can be the first to welcome the Third Millennium. Two, no prophets will be out of business on 1 January, 2000. 'Oh, you thought I meant the end of *that* millennium? No, no, mine doesn't end until the *real* millennium, which should be ... oh, about twelve years after I'm dead!'

INCIDENTALS:

ACTOR FILMOGRAPHY:
MARSHALL BELL

Marshall Bell, *Millennium*'s self-appointed Judge, is no stranger to film or TV buffs, though, in an industry only too happy to stereotype, this working actor has managed to keep his filmography incredibly diverse.

The Pretender (1996) – Warden Michaels
Operation Dumbo Drop (1995) – Pederson
Things To Do In Denver When You're Dead (1995)
– Lt Atwater
Airheads (1994) – Carl Mace
The Chase (1994) – Ari Josephson
Natural Born Killers (1994) – Deputy
The Puppet Masters (1994) – General Morgan
Silence of the Hams (1994) – Cross Dresser Agent
Air America (1990) – Ox
Dick Tracy (1990) – Lips' Cop
Total Recall (1990) – Kuato
Tucker: The Man and His Dream (1988) – Frank
The Oldest Rookie (1987) – Det Gordon Lane
Nightmare on Elm Street, Part II (1985) – Coach Schneider

CASE FILE: 'Kingdom Come'

CASE SYNOPSIS:

When a killer begins murdering priests in a highly ritualistic – and entirely too familiar – manner, Frank Black teams up with former FBI colleague, Ardis Cohen, to track the man who's already eluded them once.

KEY CITATION:

'You try to kill your faith with the tools of your own belief because of your pain, because you think God's forsaken you. You think that you can get rid of your pain by slaughtering the faith that's inside you.'

FRANK BLACK

VITAL STATISTICS:

Original US Airdate:	29/11/96
Production Number:	4C03
Written by:	Jorge Zamacona
Directed by:	Winrich Kolbe

Guest Cast:

Lindsay Crouse	Ardis Cohen
Michael Zelniker	Calloway
Laurie Murdoch	Father Schultz
Arnie Watlers	Father Brown
Terence Kelly	Detective Kerney
Ed Harrington	Marcus Crane
Wanda Wilkinson	Beatrice
Tom McBeath	Detective Romero
Jan Burrell	Jill Harned
Peter Haworth	Jack Harned
Brad Wattum	The Reverend
Alan Lehros	Jonathan Matewon

Death Toll:	3 males, one burned at the stake, one drowned, one tortured with red-hot tools. 3 other victims, all male, are known to pre-date these events. All were immolated.

CASE HISTORY:

BELL, BOOK, AND CANDLE BE DAMNED!

Today's priests, whose meagre arsenal of weapons against heretics and demons remains limited to salt, holy water, a lot of prayer, and an 'instrument' more likely to command dinner than abject terror, would be considered wimps by their medieval brethren. In fact, with

Millennium's not undeserved reputation for the visually horrific combined with the ingenuity of medieval execution, 'Kingdom Come' could easily have topped out as the season's goriest.

In a 1740 document, the English Church claimed some 'four hundreds and eleven means of putting the Accused to the Question', a further 'one hundred and nine means and variants for the Execution of the Crown's due Justice', and 'plans to address the sore lack of choice available to some more remote hamlets by the implementation of various new, less costly, and more standardized measures'. One hundred and nine ways and means of judicial execution. Modern residents of Death Row might well consider their predecessors spoiled for choice! Certainly, of those 109 methods, 'Kingdom Come' illustrated only the most tried and true.

After examining the first of this episode's victims, Ardis Cohen notes: 'Sooty residue in the air passages indicates the victim was most certainly alive when he was fastened to the stake ... carbon monoxide robbed his lungs of oxygen. When the threshold drops below 21 per cent, thankfully, you pass out.' While technically correct, her clinical statement fails to convey the numerous innovations the medieval mind conceived to circumvent that 21 per cent barrier – especially when it was a heretic, the enemy of both Church and State, who was to roast.

Anyone watching the crowd of nearly 7000 spectators who came out to see the Lord Bishop of Gloucester burned in 1555, might have wondered at the 'women a-waving their skirts and aprons whilst the men swung the shirts taken from off their backs'. An attempt to hasten the poor man's death? Not at all. The breeze created by their movement blew away the smoke, but caused the reeds used to incinerate him to burn even hotter! The results were carefully recorded by an observer whose clinical descriptions rival even Ms Cohen's. 'His face turned black, and his tongue swelled so that he could not speak, yet his lips want till they were shrunk to the gums, and he knockt his breast with his hands till one of his arms fell off, while the fat, blood and water dripped off the fingers of his other hand. Soon his nether parts were consumed and his bowels fell out.'

We can only hope most of this activity resulted from stray galvonic responses of an already dead body. However, the medieval citizen, for whom public hangings and burnings were seen as free entertainment, might be a better judge than modern minds would think and the writer entertained no doubts that the Lord Bishop was alive for '... certainly a longer while than most. God rest his soul'.

For those occasions when no crowd was present to deliver a stiff breeze, other options were available. One woman, Eleanor Elsom of Lincoln, murdered her husband and was quickly sent to the stake. Instead of the hair-shirt or scanty linen shift most women were allowed to cover themselves with, Mrs Elsom was smeared with tar. The thick substance was worked into her hair before the long coil was looped around her head to form a 'tar bonnet'. The poor woman went up like a torch long before the wood and shavings around her feet could create any significant amount of the smoke that other condemned individuals had been known to lean over and deliberately breath into their lungs. Just two years later, in Germany, four heretical priests were dressed in their own 'tar clothes' and tied to a single stake. The blaze was visible in neighboring communities.

If judgement called for a particularly nasty form of immolation, however, the executioner might opt for a different venue altogether. The stake, even in the hands of an expert, could kill much too quickly for the heretic to get out so much as an 'Amen' and, at least theoretically, the touch of the flames, a precursor to the heretic's trip to Hell, was intended to convince the wayward soul to repent before death. To ensure the victim received plenty of time to reconsider, the gridiron was a handy tool. Essentially a man-sized camp toaster, it consisted of two iron racks between which the heretic was squashed. With the gridiron hung over a low fire, a skilled questioner could keep victims alive for a considerable time by slowly cooking both sides and varying the fuels used. Of course, the courts and Church provided their own observers to make sure this was indeed an execution, not anything as vulgar as torture. The victim, however, might easily fail to make the distinction.

Whether this episode's killer simply wasn't aware of the

LINDSAY CROUSE BRINGS A PASSIONATE PRESENCE TO HER PORTRAYAL OF ARDIS COHEN, THE ONLY OTHER MEMBER OF THE GROUP KNOWN TO BE IN A FULL-TIME RELATIONSHIP

many refinements made over the past millennium, or whether he was just ready for a change after four immolations, his next choice, trial by water, was a definite reversal. Once again, though, he opted for the classic drowning scenario instead of the creative alternatives developed by both amateur and professional executions.

Perhaps because every community needed a source of water, and thus tended to settle near ponds, rivers or wells, death by drowning proved a convenient way to execute almost anyone. And, because water, like the moon, enjoys symbolic links to magic, the antithesis of organized religions, it was seen as a fitting repository for witches and heretics. As with fire, however, individual communities created their own variant of the 'death by water' scenario based on the water supply at hand.

CATCH IT? The door broken by the bird's impact, the door used for 23 of the season's 24 episodes isn't the same door seen in the pilot.

Coastal areas, especially those with distinct tidal zones, simply moved their stake from a hilltop to the beach. The unfortunate victim, tied to the post at low tide, had hours to rethink their position as they watched the water creep towards, and ultimately engulf them. To prevent the condemned from using the intervening time to continue sinning by calling on unholy alliances, cursing the executioners, or, greatest sin of all, continuing to declare their innocence, victims were often treated to the 'Witch's Scold', a cruel cage that fitted around the head and forced a piece of metal in the offender's mouth. The mouthpiece frequently incorporated spikes or razor-sharp edges that savaged the victim's tongue and palate if they attempted to speak. Not surprisingly, as they watched the water approaching, some of those staked to the beach couldn't repress their cries for help and actually died of blood loss. Even so, the good judges apparently weren't as sure of water executions as they were of death by fire, and drowning orders often incorporated precise directions including the number of times the tide was to cover the victim – like once wouldn't do it?

Inland courts, without a convenient tidal area handy, needed to be more inventive and it's from one of these small

TESTIMONY TRIVIA 5

QUESTIONS

1 What unique culinary delicacy does Frank serve Jordan?
2 What odd item of clothing was the first victim wearing?
3 What type of coin turned up at several of the crime scenes?
4 How many golf clubs did the Killer carry in his bag?
5 Who is Ardis Cohen's 'other half'?
6 What was found in the Protestant priest's stomach?
7 What was the name of the third victim's granddaughter?
8 What was the Killer's previous profession?
9 On what holiday did the Killer's family die?
10 What happened to the Killer's fingerprints?

hamlets that the scenario for the death of the fictional Rev. Marcus Crane arose. If your creek wasn't tall enough to drown a standing man, you went ahead and tied him to the stake – then threw stake and heretic into the water! While a drowning man might be saved by clinging to a piece of wood, a man tied to a stake inevitably rolls under it. The community of Salvington, whose local stream was nowhere deeper than a foot during the hotter months, nevertheless managed to drown eighteen heretics there in the summer of 1782.

Towns lucky enough to arise on the edges of deep ponds, or with a seafaring history, quickly abandoned the stake's symbolism altogether. Making use of their natural resources, while saving themselves the cost of a later burial, residents simply rowed out to the center of the pond, or into deeper offshore waters and tossed their heretic, confined in a weighted bag or attached to a length of chain ending in a heavy weight, over the side. Escaping the confining apparatus didn't really help. Mary Bourne actually clawed her way through the brim bag and back to the surface only to be confined, two days later, in 'a huge pot, the lid of which was weighted down by six men as scalding water was poured through a knotch at the rim'.

Where full submersion proved inappropriate, a number of innovative techniques arose. In India, a funnel-shaped metal collar was locked around the victim's neck, packed with cloth to muffle any screams or unwanted burbling noises, then slowly filled with water. In Greece, the victim, after being tied flat on his back to a plank, was slid headfirst under a fall of water. In Japan, a length of water-soaked linen, wrapped around the victim's head 20 or 30 times, and kept wet with the aid of a dipper, proved to be an entirely satisfactory way to suffocate a missionary deemed by his brothers to be 'too loose with his interpretation of Scripture'.

When Calloway calmly explained to victim number six, Reverend Jack Harned, that 'During the Inquisition, priests were forbidden to draw blood, so they would heat their tools red-hot. That way, the wound cauterized. No blood, no mess', he wasn't necessarily ruling out either of his former methods. What he was introducing, as his tools rested over the minister's stove, was the 'interactive' element of Spanish trials, the 'Inquisition' part of the Spanish Inquisition. Sure, having your flesh torn apart with hot irons probably was likely to, eventually, result in a long, lingering sort of death, but it wasn't nearly as impersonal as drowning or burning. As a means of extracting confessions from recalcitrant penitents, though, it topped the charts of available methods. Just as almost every village had a source of water or a convenient tree trunk to use as a stake, even the most miserable little hamlet had some metal implements and something to heat them with.

With the appearance, early in this episode, of the *san benito*, an item intrinsically connected to the Spanish Inquisition, and the recurrent appearance of Spanish pesetas, it's only fitting that the last victim be 'put to the Question' in traditional style. That Calloway apparently received as few satisfying answers as the Inquisitors he emulated was, perhaps, merely a case of history repeating itself.

NOTEBOOK:

The San Benito

Extrapolating the existence of a *san benito* from the tiny scraps of cloth left clinging to the burnt stake probably would require the services of a near-psychic investigator. While almost every form of medieval execution required the condemned to wear some outward symbol of their status, the *san benito* was distinctive even among that odd array of garments. Unlike the singed bit of stuff Frank finds at the scene, the real *san benito*, which originated during, and seems to be specific to, the Spanish Trials, was a brilliant yellow tunic, not a cloak, further embellished with hand-painted artwork that ranged from caricature to high art.

The typical scene incorporated an image of the accused surrounded by devils just waiting for the flames, another consistent part of the picture, to engulf the victim before they pounced and dragged him to Hell. The imagery was highly symbolic. The pictures on the unrepentant heretic's tunic

MEGAN GALLAGHER AND LANCE HENRIKSEN PORTRAY ONE OF TV'S MOST INTRIGUING COUPLES

featured flames leaping upwards; on the confessed, and sup-posedly repentant, heretic's shirt, the flames pointed down-ward.

Nor was the *san benito* the only item of ritualistic gar-ment worn to the stake. In many cases, a brilliant yellow hat, about a yard tall and shaped like the 'dunce cap' of school-room fame, finished off the *ensemble*. Ridiculous as all this appeared, very few would have refused to wear it. The alter-native was to be dragged along the same route, usually through the center of town, completely naked.

INCIDENTALS:

This episode aired out of order in the US due to the death of American Cardinal Bernadine. Fox felt it would be 'in poor taste' to run an episode based on the fictional murder of priests as 'the Nation mourned'. Many fans, however, won-dered if the widely reported schedule change wasn't merely an attempt by Fox to bolster the then-low ratings by putting the show back in the news.

CASE FILE: '522666'

CASE SYNOPSIS:

Frank Black's investigation of an apparently motiveless bombing quickly leads him to reject the larger taskforce's initial assumption that a terrorist group is at work inside American borders. His theory is proven in dramatic style when the Bomber singles him out as not only his sounding board, but the object of his next explosion! Finding this killer, who follows none of the 'rules', will require all Frank's empathy, a commodity in increasingly short supply as the Bomber sets a break-neck pace.

KEY CITATION:

'I feel your "work" is about waiting,
anticipating the moment, the terror created.
Playing so long in the mind, the fantasy
becomes dull. The only moment worth
a damn, the only "arousal" is the
element of fire.'

FRANK BLACK

VITAL STATISTICS:

Original US Airdate:	11/22/96
Production Number:	4C05
Written by:	Glen Morgan and James Wong
Directed by:	David Nutter

Guest Cast:

Terry O'Quinn	Peter Watts
Joe Chrest	Raymond Dees
Sam Anderson	Pierson
Robert Lewis	Sullivan
William MacDonald	Agent Nolan
Ed Striedinger	Agent Mills
Roger Barns	Agent Smith
Claudine Grant	Agent Wallace
Hiro Kanagawa	Agent Yung
Peter Bryant	Officer Riley
Deryl Hayes	Officer Stanton
Death Toll:	18, by explosion

CASE HISTORY:

A TWISTED BOMBER OR A BOMBER WITH A TWIST? Even before the Millennium Group

beeped Frank, before the opening credits for '522666' rolled, trailers for this episode recalled some of America's most horrific bombings. Ads flashed 'OKLAHOMA CITY' and 'WORLD TRADE CENTER' at potential viewers while inviting them 'inside the mind of a terrorist'. And the comparisons continued as soon as the episode opened. Even as Frank packs his bag, a TV announcer sums it up with, ' ... when an event like this occurs in the nation's capital, the possibility of a terrorist attack cannot be dismissed.' Yet, despite all the hype, neither the Oklahoma City bombing nor the World Trade Center scenario fits the fictional bomber's activities. *Millennium*'s bomber had an agenda, but not one that any of America's prominent bombers would recognize.

At 9:02 am, on 19 April, 1995, the front was blown off the Alfred P Murrah Federal Building in Oklahoma City. Dozens died, including children who were supposedly safely sheltered in a ground floor day-care. Even in the midst of the chaos, even before the emergency response teams flew into action, law enforcement officials had absolutely no doubt that, whoever the bombers turned out to be, they had *reasons* for picking a Federal Building, for staging their explosion on 19 April, the anniversary of the destruction of the Branch Davidian Complex, and for choosing Oklahoma City, literally in America's heartland. And, unlike the taskforce assembled to address the fictional bomber on *Millennium*, the joint investigators in Oklahoma remained firmly convinced they were dealing with a group, not an individual. When Timothy McVeigh and Terry Nichols, arrested and charged in the Oklahoma City bombing, went under the investigative and media microscopes, they certainly seemed to 'fit the profile'.

HENRIKSEN'S PLAYED A MULTITUDE OF ROLES, BUT IT'S HARD TO IMAGINE ANYONE ELSE AS FRANK BLACK

Both men participated in, and sympathized with, the militia-styled groups which produce most attacks on government installations. Within that subculture, the 19 April tragedy at Waco is a landmark date. Planning a bombing to coincide with the anniversary makes a twisted sort of sense, reflecting some sort of history, some *reason*, a motive. Raymond Dees had no such affiliations, no 'fallen comrades' to recall. Nor did his target make *political* sense. Why attack a British pub? For as long as the British and American governments remain on amicable terms, the pub bombing serves none of the multiple 'motives' that might appeal to men with McVeigh's or Nichols' background.

Just as Dees and the Oklahoma City bombers fell miles apart on philosophical grounds, so were the tools they chose. The bomb left in front of the Murrah Building, nothing more than a truck stuffed with fuel oil and fertilizer, is, technically and 'artistically', as far removed from the *Millennium* bomber's intricate explosives as kindergarten hand-paintings are from Rembrandts. In fact, some experts remain surprised that the Oklahoma City device exploded at all! An almost identical setup prepared by a disgruntled Los Angeles native intent on blowing up the local IRS building, simply fizzled out. The car bomb left outside the Irish Parliament in August, 1996, sputtered for a few moments then extinguished itself, leaving nothing more serious than a foul odour. Simplistic as these devices are, however, when they do work, they do exactly what they're designed to do – maim, destroy, and kill.

Raymond Dees's creations, on the other hand, capable of toppling a man standing in a concrete building across the street while leaving the bomber himself without a scratch, would require a touch so elegant that even Fabergé would be envious. For the Oklahoma City killers, car bombs, or any other sort of bomb, are merely the cheapest, and most accessible, weapons they can find or build that remain capable of inflicting the degree of damage they craved. If bathtubs could have made bigger holes, or killed more people, well then, they'd have thrown bathtubs! For Dees, who waxed so eloquent about his portraits of blood and glass, the car bomb would have been much too broad a brush.

Likewise, it's equally certain that the men who parked their bomb on the second level of the World Trade Center garage on 26 February, 1993, weren't 'artists' either. Politics is a public business, and so is politically-motivated terrorism. The bigger the bomb, the more media coverage it's likely to receive, which is, of course, the goal of a political bomber. Like the Oklahoma City bombers, the New York City group followed their own political agenda, one that didn't include hanging about to admire the view when one could be better occupied at the nearest phone or postbox claiming responsibility for the blast. As Black noted, 'Political terrorists would be far from the scene. He [Dees] was here, watching.'

Political activists, regardless of anarchist leanings, display an amazingly well-developed sense of self-preservation! True, the suicide-bomber, the modern version of WWII's kamikaze pilot, still surfaces from time to time. Yet, the vast majority of political terrorists prefer handing their deadly packages over to unsuspecting innocents or, killing several birds with one stone, unwitting, but inconvenient, members of their own organizations! One bomber tucked his organization's explosives into his mother-in-law's luggage before generously offering her a ride to the airport and slipping her skycap an extra fiver 'to make sure everything gets off safely'. But even he didn't wait around, peering towards the clouds, hoping to see the flash.

CATCH IT? In the opening scenes, a television announcer is caught mid-speech as Frank channel-surfs: '...calls it one of the best new shows of the season. Sundays, after football.' In less than two full sentences, they manage to work a little self-reference to Fox's new acquisition, *NFL Football*, the new slot for *The X-Files* and, of course, *Millennium* itself!

Political bombers are practical people. Bombers who hang out at ground zero run two equally unneccesary risks. Firstly, bombing, in the hands of those who learn their craft from a subculture book or magazine, isn't an exact science. A stray piece of glass, a crumbling wall, even a panic-stricken motorist, could end the bomber's career pretty quickly. Secondly, for maximum effect, bombs tend to get planted in heavily-peopled locations instead of cornfields. Where there are crowds of people, it's all too possible that at least one of them will remember the guy who left the package or parked the van. Whether from cowardice or common sense, most bombers get as far from the crime scene as possible before detonation.

References to IRA bomb codes, Middle Eastern 'freedom fighters', ZOG and *The Turner Diaries* aside, *Millennium*'s version of a terrorist just doesn't mesh with the sort of organized political underground stressed in all those advertisements.

TESTIMONY TRIVIA 6

QUESTIONS

1 What bar did 'KABOOM' blow up?
2 What was written on the Taskforce door?
3 How many backups did the Bomber build into his first bomb?
4 What was distinctive about the Bomber's briefcase clasp?
5 What's Frank's cellular phone number?
6 To what cartoon character did Frank compare the bomber?
7 Which organization did the Bomber mimic by using phone tones?
8 What business was the focus of the Bomber's second attack?
9 What did Jack Pierson ask his snipers to aim for?
10 Raymond Dees had a military record. What was his serial number?

Instead, '522666' gave us perhaps the oddest criminal combination ever to hit the airwaves. In intense, rasping tones, Frank Black portrays a bomber in complete opposition to the political terrorist: 'He was excited, anticipating what was about to happen. And, at midnight last night, he got his release.' Just in case there was any doubt about what sort of 'release' Frank described, he and the taskforce leader turn up what might be politely described as 'a substantial DNA sample' in a napkin discarded at the site just before Peter Watts starts throwing theories of sexual transference about! Stirring a little 'suicide by cop' scenario into the already confused, and confusing, character of Raymond Dees did, however, accomplish the near impossible. Despite sacrificing something of the reality the show otherwise strives to present, the *Millennium* staff created a compelling, suspenseful hour of television peopled by characters capable of stumping and intriguing even jaded modern audiences.

NOTEBOOK:

Hoist By Their Own Petard

When the Taskforce Leader says that 'after Centennial Park', they don't dare arrest anyone for being a hero, the reference is, of course, to the explosion of a pipe bomb in Centennial Park at the height of the 1996 Atlanta Olympics. Literally overnight, Richard Jewell went from being the 'hero' who'd spotted the suspicious bag to the man with the the the apartment most likely to have a couple of FBI agents wandering about it carrying evidence bags.

Why? Probably because the FBI, who used to be a 'just the facts' type of agency, now include behavorial sciences as a routine part of the criminal analysis process. Years of shared investigative experience, now being organized into specific observations and applied to similar cases, proves that certain types of criminal operate solely to nab more than the average person's 'fifteen minutes of fame'.

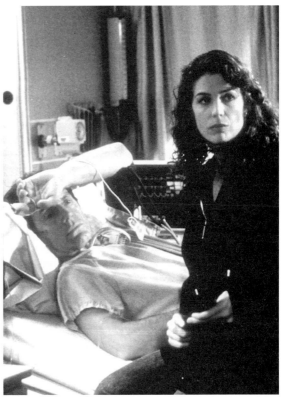

Sadly, because so many perpetrators find ways to worm their way into the investigation of their crimes, everything from hanging out at the local 'cop bar' to eavesdrop, to actually reporting their own crimes and then 'keeping in touch out of curiosity', Richard Jewell, and anyone else in the same situation, would almost automatically come under at least casual investigation. As Susan Smith, who drowned her two sons and then went on TV to

IT TOOK TWO EXPLOSIONS TO SEND AN EXHAUSTED FRANK BLACK TO BED

tearfully beg the 'car-jacker' to return her children, proved, it's quickly becoming difficult to separate the victims from the perpetrators.

Making matters worse for Richard Jewell, he coincidentally fell into two more 'suspect' categories. He was a volunteer security officer, a position favoured by 'police freaks' for its authority factor. Jewell also appeared in several interviews for prestigious news programs. While being a volunteer, answering questions and calling in an apparently suspicious situation to the proper authorities are all innocent enough activities under normal circumstances, amid the pressures of an ongoing inquiry, such seemingly irrelevant items easily begin looking like part of an all-too-familiar pattern.

Richard Jewell was cleared of suspicion during an FBI press conference.

Of course, Richard Jewell wasn't on the scene at two different explosions.

INCIDENTALS:

This episode gave viewers their first peek into Frank Black's closet, just enough to confirm that, as everyone was already beginning to suspect, every article of clothes owned by Frank Black is some shade of gray! Must make laundry days easy.

☐

Mr Henriksen does most of his own stunts, including little things like jumping out of the way of sFX explosions, even if that means several physical takes for each scene, as happened on this episode. It comes pretty naturally as it was accomplished stuntman, TK, who convinced Henriksen that acting wasn't a half-bad career.

CASE FILE: 'Blood Relatives'

CASE SYNOPSIS:

Using Frank's profile, Seattle's finest have managed to capture a suspect believed to have savagely murdered and mutilated at least three people. Frank should be happy. Instead, he finds it more and more difficult to reconcile Catherine's humanistic profile, a picture of one of society's 'lost' children, with a killer with a predilection for the recently bereaved.

KEY CITATION:

'No one showed him how to connect with
the world. Odd as this is going to sound,
going to funerals is his attempt.'

CATHERINE BLACK

VITAL STATISTICS:

Original US Airdate: 12/06/96

Production Number: 4C06
  Written by: Chip Johannessen
  Directed by: Jim Charleston

Guest Cast:
  Sean Six   James Dickerson
  John Fleck   Connors
  Stephen James Lang   Detective Giebelhouse
  Terry O'Quinn   Peter Watts
  Nicole Parker   Greer Cort
  Diana Stevan   Mrs Cort
  Bob Morrissey   Charles Cort

Death Toll: 2, female, stabbed to death

CASE HISTORY:

WHEN IT ISN'T ALL IN YOUR HEAD

Despite Frank Black's impressive ability to reconstruct the action at a crime scene, his fleeting, disjointed visions aren't likely to convict any perpetrators. Recognizing the need to include realistic portrayals of criminal investigations, most *Millennium* episodes feature the collection of hard, physical, forensic evidence. In fact, Jim Penseyres, Peter Watts and Cheryl Andrews, the most frequently seen members of the Millennium Group, all appear to have backgrounds in some area of forensic evidence collection. Even Frank Black, the 'soft scientist' in the Group, displays an unusual amount of concern to avoid contamination of crime scenes. Has an episode gone by which hasn't featured him carefully closing the front of his jacket and shoving his hands dead in his pockets? Of course, considering the number of technologies alluded to, if not actually demonstrated onscreen, Frank's concern hardly seems misplaced.

In this episode, physical evidence provides numerous pointers to the Killer's identity, though, when Peter Watts claims to have retrieved fingerprints from a submerged buckle, even Giebelhouse seems incredulous. Watts's response, 'we've lifted prints off of bones buried fifty years' may have been pushing the limits just a bit. Fingerprints typically last longer in warm, humid conditions than in cool surroundings. However, in an experiment on papyrus scrolls thousands of

LT ROBERT 'BLETCH' BLETCHER (BILL SMITROVICH) ALWAYS SEEMS TO BE JUST THAT STEP BEHIND FRANK

years old, forsensic technicians managed to bring up prints belonging to the writer! Obviously, some extraordinary techniques were required, but the processes available to investigators become more refined almost daily.

In the area of fingerprinting alone, technicians now have dozens of options for retrieving visible or hidden prints. Everyone's seen the dusting techniques, the little jars of variously colored powders, some of them magnetic, blown or brushed onto everything from glass to garden hoses. In addition to dusting, however, there's also spraying, fuming and dipping, and that's only for starters. There's also laser treatment, X-rays, fluorescence, and even fungal bloom!

The buckle recovered from the pebble-strewn lake bed in 'Blood Relations' certainly isn't the most unlikely surface ever to be tested. A plain metal surface, relatively undisturbed despite its brief immersion in fresh water, *can* be treated. After being allowed to air-dry, a raw metal surface can be subjected to small particle reagent, sprayed with cyanoacrylate, and even dusted with one of the non-magnetic powders. Any one of those techniques could reasonably be expected to turn up a useable print, and, if none of them worked, a visible image might still be found using fluorescent lighting. While some surfaces present more problems than others, the list of surfaces from which a print can't be lifted is getting shorter each day. Skin, which just twenty years ago was considered an impossible surface is, using the same materials available then, a regular source of information.

Of course, prints aren't the only evidence used by regular law enforcement agencies, or by the consultants sometimes brought in on difficult investigations. When Frank sends Peter Watts back to the lab, looking for a 'message' that no one can find, it's forensic botany that eventually connects the first victim to the others. The pollen grains caught between strands of cloth in this episode, like the cranberry seeds found embedded in a sock in 'The Judge', illustrate the type of trace evidence forensic biologists actively seek. In addition to suggesting where a victim was physically, spores, seeds, leaf fragments or other vegetable debris help fix the time of death or abduction. For example, as every hay fever sufferer knows, various plants drop their seeds or spores in a predictable pattern. Rayweed plants inflict their particular brand of misery for a limited time, generally completing their reproductive cycle before grass, but after cotton poplar.

Soil analysis, also known as forensic geology, is closely linked to forensic botany in that both are dependent on the technician being able to identify the sample, then judge where it is mostly likely to have come from. As with many other forms of physical evidence, law enforcement officials don't expect a perfect 'match'. What they require, and what both botany and geology can deliver, is the answer to 'did this sample come from location X?'. If the evidence is negative, that is it eliminates a suspect, it's said to be 'exculpetory'. Exculpetory evidence, which can eliminate suspects and free investigators to pursue more likely trails, is always welcome, even if it is simultaneously disappointing and frustrating.

Of course, some evidence is as useful in identifying specific individuals as it is in eliminating them. The forensic dentistry scene which leads the Millennium Group to Eedo Bolow in 'Gehenna', is, taken point for point, a mini-lecture in the process actual forensic dentists undertake when asked to help identify an unknown victim. Given a complete set of teeth, and accurate, up-to-date dental records, dentistry can provide identifications as positive as any physical fingerprint. Amalgams used to create fillings, the relative sophistication of processes like bonding or crowning, even the material used in creating dentures or braces can reveal the location of the work, the time frame in which the work was completed, and, in some cases even provide clues to the victim's state of health when the work was done.

BLOOPER! Even if there was some explanation for the fact that Tina's pebble landed in water barely deep enough to plop, but apparently deep enough to totally submerge a full-grown woman, it doesn't explain the white rim at the bottom of the underwater shots!

The bombings in '522666' would have provided a real-life lab with enough evidence to keep it busy for months. Something called the 'chemical signature', the specific combination of materials found in a given batch of explosives can be so precise that investigators need only trace it back to the manufacturer, then forward to the purchaser. Likewise, unless the triggering devices are homemade, even a few numbers on any item used in its construction can lead through the same back and forth trail as the explosives.

No discussion of forensics, real or fictional, would be complete without some reference to blood evidence. *Millennium*, surprisingly, *hasn't* fallen prey to the 'weekly DNA test' trap. While numerous cop shows, even hospital programs, feature 'miracle labs' that, somehow, manage to return full blood work-up, including DNA results that require weeks to obtain in the real world, *Millennium*'s use of blood evidence has, so far, been limited to what a normally-equipped lab, or an observant investigator, could come up with in the timespan of the episodes. In 'Dead Letters', Frank is quick to point out the blood splatter pattern to his agitated partner. Blood splatter evidence has been well documented since 1971 and requires only that the examiner be an observant investigator. In 'Weeds', Cheryl Andrews returns preliminary blood-typing and screening, enough to confirm that the victims hadn't ingested their own blood, but without any of the bells and whistles that might have had the community council demanding everyone in town submit to a blood work-up to find a killer with some rare blood factor. The tight scheduling of 'Weeds', one of the factors providing the episode's punch, would have fallen completely flat if significant blood evidence popped up within the 72-hour time-frame established in the opening minutes.

When any type of information is available at any time to anyone, fictional investigators become little more than lecturers. Used realistically, as has been the case with *Millennium*, forensics adds an element of anticipation, even frustration, to the dramatic mix.

NOTEBOOK:

Crazy Little Thing Called Time

If criminal investigations and scriptwriting share one peculiarity, it's an obsession with recalling who was where when. In scripts, an assortment of scene header tags like ' — NIGHT', ' — DAY', ' — MOMENTS LATER', and ' — SUNSET' keep track of timelines. Detectives create multiple-branch flow charts and minute-by-minute schedules to account for the movements of victims, perpetrators and witnesses. Given this fixation with timing, you'd expect a script *about* crime to pay particular attention to all the details. Instead, no two characters in 'Blood Relatives' could seem to agree on the day, much less time, of death of any of the victims!

Take this sequence for example. Mr Cort takes great exception to being separated from his dead wife's body for *three days*. Catherine is suitably shocked. Bletch expresses

TESTIMONY TRIVIA 7

QUESTIONS

1 What was Jeff Cort's birthday? _
2 What did Frank find in the bottom of the grave?
3 Something was stolen from Jeff's casket. What?
4 What was the real Ray Bell 'famous' for?
5 What message was found on the victims' bodies?
6 Where did James Dickerson hide out?
7 Name Dickerson's half-brother.
8 Where did Dickerson live after getting out of jail?
9 Which section of the paper was Dickerson's favorite?
10 Where did Frank find Dickerson's mother and the killer?

his remorse at the situation. Then, when Frank and Greer re-enact events at the wake, Frank refers to the theft of Jeff's pin happening 'yesterday'. Talk about missing time!

The situation doesn't improve as the action moves along either. When Frank presents Bletcher and Giebelhouse with Jeff Cort's obituary, and a news article on the real Ray Bell, he says, 'This is the obituary of the boy who died. It appeared two days ago.' By this time, Mrs Cort has already been in the morgue for four days! And, why would the Cort family arrange an obituary that wouldn't appear until two days *after* the funeral anyway? To compound the confusion, in the same scene, Frank adds, '*Last night*, he crossed the line into murderous violence ...' Evidently Frank forgot he'd been working this case for several days already!

Nor is it an isolated dialogue problem afflicting Frank Black alone. Even the props contribute to the confusion. The first time James Dickerson peruses the obituaries, he reads of the death of William J 'Jack' McDougall on Sunday, 15 November, 1996. As the episode closes, and James is once again working his way through the death notices, he circles the name of Michael John Peyson whose memorial service will be held on 22 November. Even if McDougall's family managed to get their notice in on the same day Jack died, and

Dickerson was only interested in that day's events, seven days simply aren't sufficient to account for the time taken to solve the case.

In a genre that doesn't encourage the audience to actively think about on-screen events, that doesn't issue an implicit invitation to solve the case before the Hero, time is merely a means of separating one scene from another. In a show that's essentially a mystery, such inattention to major details is disturbing.

INCIDENTALS:

ACTOR FILMOGRAPHY:

SEAN SIX

Sean Six, may be one of the hardest guest stars for fans to place, one of those 'the voice is familiar, but I can't place the face' situations. And, no wonder, Sean Six's most familiar role, as Buck Francisco in both film and television versions of the cult favorite *Alien Nation* has always appeared in the standard Newcomer make-up, which enlarges the head, removes all traces of hair, and then dapples the entire skull with red spots.

Alien Nation: Millennium (1996)
Alien Nation: The Enemy Within (1996)
Alien Nation: Body and Soul (1995)
Alien Nation: Dark Horizon (1994)
Alien Nation: 'The Series' (1989)
Alien Nation (1989)

CASE FILE: 'The Well-Worn Lock'

CASE SYNOPSIS:

A twenty-year-old case of child sexual abuse loses none of its emotional power, or danger, as Catherine Black pursues one of the 'pillars' of Seattle society in a high-stakes bid to ensure the safety of a second generation. Frank, in the unusual position of being on the outside looking in, can only watch as his wife takes the fight to the courtroom while the rapist takes it back to where it started, the middle-class home of another young girl.

KEY CITATION:

'I've seen cases like these come through here now and again. Nobody wants them, not even the good ones – and this isn't one.'

ADA RHONDA PRESHUTSKI

VITAL STATISTICS:

Original US Airdate:	12/20/96
Production Number:	4C07
Written by:	Chris Carter
Directed by:	Ralph Hemecker

Guest Cast:

Paul Dooley	Joe Bangs
Michelle Joyner	Connie Bangs
Sheila Moore	Clea Bangs
Shaina Tianne Unger	Sara Bangs
J Douglas Stewart	Larry Bangs
Lenore Zann	Ruthie Bangs
Campbell Lane	Joe's Attorney
Steve Oatway	The Judge
Christine Dunford	ADA Rhonda Preshutski

Death Toll:	No deaths

CASE HISTORY:

VICTIM SERVICES

Jack Meredith isn't the only one wondering what the heck a Clinical Social Worker is, or just which services the Victim Services Division supplies. With luck, most of us won't need to know. But, for the estimated 367,000 people who pass through the over-worked and under-paid hands of the numerous Victim Services divisions across the United States, this relatively new resource has been, in many cases, a literal life saver. Within a judicial system that's frequently more terrifying to victims than perpetrators, Victim Services provides clients with a secure, confidential and informative retreat from the legalese of the courtroom and the clinical detachment of the hospitals that so many pass through.

Responding to the incredible variety of atrocities, both physical and emotional, which humans devise to inflict on each other, Victim Services supplies a diverse range of professional information, assistance and support.

Few victims comprehend the compartmentalized nature of the legal system. The Clinical Social Worker is the victim's guide. In addition to explaining who the bewildering array of faces belong to, why they all require their own individual hearing of the victim's statement – regardless of how many times it's already been told – walking victims through courtrooms, preparing their clients for the business side of court proceedings, and helping them prepare for the difficult process of rendering their own statements, the case worker is also the victim's advocate. It's the Victim Services representative who speaks for the victim. In both 'The Well-Worn Lock' and 'Wide Open', it's Catherine Black who buffers Connie Bangs and her young sister/daughter, as well as the traumatized Patricia Highsmith, from the system trying to 'help' them. In 'Blood Relatives', Catherine steps into the information breach developing between the bereaved Cort family and the Seattle Police Department. Though none of the Victim Services personnel interviewed for this article had ever actually held a victim's hand throughout their testimony, they concede it's an accurate symbol of their jobs, one they've frequently wished could become reality.

Acting as liaison officers with the society *outside* the courtroom, with the community's existing support facilities, Victim Services personnel ensure their clients receive whatever additional support they need. It may be an immediate need, such as physical shelter for battered children, or the start of long-term processes like rape counselling. In areas without community-based support, Victim Services bears an even heavier responsibility – if they manage to worm the extra funding and personnel from a chronically over-burdened system. The goal is simple, to prepare the victim for the upcoming ordeal of a courtroom appearance, for the delivery of a Victim Impact Statement if one is required during the penalty phase of a trial, or for the equally challenging return to everyday living.

MICHELLE JOYNER AND MEGAN GALLAGHER TURN IN MASTERFUL PERFORMANCES IN 'THE WELL-WORN LOCK'

And, it's not only victims who need education. So does the legal system itself, a system that, until recently, provided more judicial protection to alleged perpetrators than *victims*! Until Victim Services pointed out the inappropriateness of the situation, several small court buildings housed victims and their assailants in the same room before court sessions began. Small wonder the victims entering the courtroom appeared shaken and unsure to the juries and judges hearing their cases!

Governments, the real law makers, also come under scrutiny by VS personnel. While Victim Services attempts to represent each client as a distinct individual with specific needs, VS employees are also in a unique position to appreciate and record the needs victims have in common. In that broader role, they argue for victim rights at all levels of government, educate the voting public on victim issues, and suggest mechanisms to ease the communication process between victims and law enforcement personnel. Innovative reporting systems that keep victims apprised of the progress of their cases have come from Victim Services initiatives, as have improved protocols for the handling of rape, battery and abuse victims in the cold confines of medical facilities.

Taking the cause of the victim into the community, many Clinical Social Workers serve as educators, orienting groups to the difficulties victims encounter in their transition back to their previous lives, or into new circumstances.

Needless to say, VS personnel face pressure from a multitude of sources. In 'The Well-Worn Lock', Catherine encounters political pressure from local government, less-than-subtle warnings from the police department, disinterest from an ADA, and open hostility from the victim's mother. Unfortunately, that part of the picture is all too realistic. Adding to the difficulties inherent in becoming the liaison between all those official authorities are the ever-present expectations of the victims themselves. Though most Victim Services personnel don't perform long-term counselling, there's a concerted effort to keep Social Worker and client together for the duration of, at least, the legal portion of their ordeal. With trials taking longer and longer to find a space on the docket, that process can be lengthy, much more than the five months portrayed in 'The Well-Worn Lock', and, as more cases come in, the workload of any single Clinical Social Worker can quickly exceed several hundred.

So, where do these paragons of virtue come from? And what do they take away from their jobs? Most begin with a degree in either a Social or Behavioral Science. Familiarity with the local judicial system is a necessity, one usually satisfied by spending considerable portions of their free time in the courtroom and in on-the-job training before becoming eligible for case work. Ideally, an orientation process of four to six months allows new employees to become familiar with the resources and limitations of their own region – ideally.

Since 1985, when the California State University (Fresno) instigated a Victim Services Certificate Program, further study, directed specifically at the issues of victim rights and other practical topics, many VS personnel also participate in this, or similar, training. Some go even further, taking a Bachelor of Science Degree in Criminology with a concentration of study in Victimology. The Certificate Program is typically an intense 180-hour course of studies designed to provide all the skills required to work effectively with crime victims. The Bachelor program is multidisciplinary, drawing on the exper-

CARTER WAS
FORTUNATE TO
ATTRACT TWO
CONSUMMATE
PROFESSIONALS TO
HIS DARK NEW
PROGRAM

tise of sociologists, psychologists, lawyers and members of the criminal investigative branches of local, state and federal law enforcement agencies. Current and ex-FBI agents frequently address graduating classes, suggesting strategies to help victims help themselves in the courtroom. While the Certificate programs focus almost soley on the victim, graduates of the Bachelor programs also gain considerable insight into the behavior of criminals.

And the rewards for years of study, difficult working conditions, and emotionally-draining day-to-day work? Whatever else is may be, it's certainly not financial. Salaries vary with location and experience, but few members of the Victim Services staff earn much more than an experienced secretary. Yet, surprisingly, statistics indicate Clinical Social Workers

TESTIMONY TRIVIA 8

QUESTIONS

1   What film is the Bangs family enjoying in the opening scenes?
2   What is Connie doing when she's picked up by the police?
3   What's Catherine's job title?
4   Name one of Connie's siblings.
5   What company did Joe Bangs operate?
6   How did Catherine prevent Joe Bangs's escape?
7   What was the original charge against Bangs?
8   For what department does Catherine work?
9   What does Connie throw into the sluiceway?
10 Who did Jordan think Frank should protect her mom from?

remain the *least* likely of any professional group to 'burn out'. While doctors typically spend between five and seven years in any one position, lawyers a mere four to five, Clinical Social Workers average more than ten years before switching locales. Nor are they as susceptible to the marital stress afflicting those in the judicial system. Good news for Catherine and Frank!

Though most *Millennium* episodes to date emphasize the wall Frank Black erects between his work and his family life, especially evident in Catherine's tentative forays into his basement office, it's Catherine who spends her days among the victims of the killers and sadists Frank tracks! Even in the first twelve episodes, Catherine and Frank's talents have proven complementary. It's Catherine, dealing with a horrified Annie Tisman in 'The Judge', who discovers the first important link between the crime and the criminal. In 'Blood Relatives', her analysis of a suspect's diaries is the first hint that all isn't as it appears, her insights that lead Frank to understanding.

In the 'Pilot' and 'Gehenna', Frank *chooses* to hide the photographs from Catherine, but she's certainly no stranger to evil. In both 'Wide Open' and this episode, 'The Well-Worn Lock', it's Catherine, not Frank, who deals with the victims on a day-to-day basis. If Frank's facility is to understand the mind of the Killer, it appears Catherine's facility is to grasp the mind of the Victim.

NOTEBOOK:

Violence In The Mind's Eye

When *Millennium* first aired, its gory images shocked anyone expecting Chris Carter's new show to be an *X-File* clone. Considering the condition of the program's first victims, emaciated people, buried alive, their mouths and eyes sewn shut, their mutilated hands leaving bloody trailers on the inside of the coffins, fluid bags of their own blood sloshing at their feet, that particular criticism proved accurate and, as the cast and crew had been saying all along, 'the program isn't for everyone'.

The charge that *Millennium* would turn out to be a 'serial killer of the week' program, however, has proven completely unfounded. Certainly, there are killers, but, there are killers in nearly every episode of nearly every cop show ever to hit the airwaves. There are violent acts, victims, and terror of one type or another in every episode. Still, just as most of the gore in Carter's previous series occurred off-screen, or was merely hinted at by flickering shadows of the action cast against convenient walls and mirrors, *Millennium* rarely shows vicious acts themselves. Instead, it presents audiences with the *results* of terrorism, or sadism, or the more everyday sort of abuse of 'The Well-Worn Lock'.

Any number of straight 'dramatic' television programs, and dozens of movies, have tackled incest, home violence and child abuse. Yet *Millennium*, renowned for blood and gore, hovering all too close to the horror genre, took those same issues and produced what is undoubtedly one of the most moving and powerful hours of television ever – all without showing a single drop of blood.

A N S W E R S

1   *Miracle on 34th Street*
2   Walking the center line
3   Clinical Social Worker
4   Larry or Ruth, two points if you knew both
5   Glen Rock Realty
6   She ran the Jeep out in front of his car
7   Reckless child endangerment
8   Victim Services
9   The deadbolt from her bedroom door
10 Lt Bletcher

YOUR SCORE:

What the writers of this extraordinary episode apparently realized, and certainly incorporated into 'The Well-Worn Lock', is the power that anticipation, suggestion, and imagination have, not only in the victimization depicted on screen, but in the minds of viewers.

Alfred Hitchcock once advised young filmmakers not to reveal the terror behind the locked door too early: 'Once the heroine opens the door, once you've shown the horror, the film is over.'

Looking back at *Millennium's* first season, few will have forgotten the terror of this episode, an episode where no one died, and at least two people were rescued.

INCIDENTALS:

ACTOR FILMOGRAPHY:

PAUL DOOLEY

Like so many of the actors invited to the *Millennium* set this season, Paul Dooley, an actor's actor, arrived with an impressive list of credits and turned in a stunning performance.

Clockwatchers (1997) – Bud Chapman
Telling Lies in America (1997) – Father Norton
Evolver (1995) – Jerry Briggs
Grace Under Fire – John Shirley (1994–5)
Tales of the City (1993) – Herb Tolliver
Cooperstown (1993) – Sid Wiggins
My Boyfriend's Back (1993) – Big Chuck
Perry Mason: The Case of the Heartbroken Bride (1992)
The Player (1992) – Himself!
Flashback (1990) – Stark
Strange Brew (1983) – Claude Elsinore
Breaking Away (1979) – Dad
Slap Shot (1977) – Hyannisport Announcer

▶ ▶ ▶ ▶ ▶ ▶

RESIDENTS OF THE YELLOW HOUSE

MEGAN GALLAGHER:

MEGAN GALLAGHER AS THE BEWITCHING CATHERINE BLACK

Megan Gallagher, born in Reading, Pennsylvania, on 6 February, 1960, decided she wanted to act before she started primary school, and, when she entered New York's eminent Julliard School, nothing much had changed – luckily for *Millennium* fans. She went on to work with John Houseman's Acting Company and moved to Los Angeles where she fed stray cats and took her share of casting calls. Roles came, some of which, like her spot on *Hill Street Blues*, became recurring roles and ensured her wider exposure. Before long, she was working regularly – regularly enough to be particular about the roles she chose to take on. The fact that Chris Carter had already created *The X-Files's* Dana Scully, one of the most intriguing women currently on television, was a deciding factor in her signing on as Catherine Black. While several episodes have hinted at the potential inherent in the character, and a few episodes like 'The Well-Worn Lock' and 'Wide Open' have allowed her considerable professional scope, audiences are still waiting for the actress's potential and the character's to finally come together permanently.

MEGAN GALLAGHER AS
MRS VEIL IN 'NOWHERE
MAN'

FILMOGRAPHY

Crosscut (1996) – Anna Hennessey
ER – Cathy Snyder (1996)
Breaking Free (1995) – Annie Sobel
Nowhere Man – Alyson Veil (1995)
Trade Off (1995) – Karen Hughes
The Birds II: Land's End (1994) – Joanna Hocken
Star Trek: Deep Space Nine – Nurse Garland (1993)
The Larry Sanders Show – Jeannie Sanders (1992)
Pacific Station (1991) – Det. Sandy Calloway
And Then She Was Gone (1991) – Laura McKillin
The Ambulance (1990) – Sandra Malloy
Champagne Charlie (1989) – Pauline
China Beach – DJ Wayloo Marie Holmes (1988–9)
The Slap Maxwell Story – Judy Ralston (1987)
George Washington (1984) – Peggy Shippen
Hill Street Blues – Tina Russo (1981)
Dallas – Louella (1979–81)

BRITTANY TIPLADY

Though she obviously doesn't bring a lot of experience to the *Millennium* set, Brittany Tiplady plays a pivotal character as Jordan Black, the precocious child who may yet be gifted with some of her father's unusual abilities. When the evil which Frank Black is so vehemently fighting is contrasted with Brittany Tiplady's brilliant smile and wide, curious eyes, then the central facts of the Blacks' lives become self-evident. And, without this delightful young actress, The Yellow House would be an empty place after all.

THE BLACK FAMILY WITH TV'S FASTEST-GROWING DOG!

LANCE HENRIKSEN AS
BISHOP IN 'ALIENS'

LANCE HENRIKSEN

In an era when so many leading men's bios wouldn't fill the
back of a milk carton, watching Lance Henriksen, who brings
the equivalent of several lifetimes' worth of rich experience to
his varied roles, has been a rare treat. And an interesting life
it's been since 5 May, 1943 – even without the extra glitz of
living the Hollywood life.

In the two years before they divorced, his parents were
busy people. His mother was a model/dancer while his
father juggled boxing, writing and sailing. Though he was
essentially self-raised and self-educated, Henriksen left
home when he was just twelve. He'd apparently inherited his
folks' love of variety. In between a number of youthful jail
stints, Henriksen himself shrimped, picked fruit, cobbled
together a number of carpentry jobs, learned to fly, and, yes,
even acted in a Lee Marvin film for which he received the

LANCE HENRIKSEN AS WALLY SCHIRRA IN 'THE RIGHT STUFF'

grand sum of five dollars. If nothing else, the illiterate kid from NY was learning more about the country he was constantly hitch-hiking across, and about people, than he could have done in any acting class. Still, on the advice of stunt-director Rex Rossi, Henriksen was giving more serious thought to a career on stage or screen.

On discovering that he was still too young for acceptance into the acting school of his choice, the Actor's Studio of New York, he widened his horizon a little more and, like his father, took to the sea. There was the stint aboard a Swedish freighter, the time spent tooling around the Caribbean under real sail, and then the three-year hitch spent in the real Navy before spending two more years on the water with the Merchant Marine.

Then, after considering a job painting scenery, he plunged straight into acting instead, taking a stage role that reflected his personal knowledge of the sea. From then on, he's managed to be a working film actor. It took some long conversations before he was coaxed away from the big screen but, having seen him as Frank Black, few people can imagine anyone else in the role.

FILMOGRAPHY

Profile for Murder (1997) – Adrian Cross

Aurora: Operation Intercept (1995) – William Stenghel

Baja (1995) – Burns

Dead Man (1995) – Cole Wilson

Felony (1995) – Taft

Gunfighter's Moon (1995) – Frank Morgan

Nature of the Beast (1995) – Jack Powell

The Outpost (1995) – Stockton

Powder (1995) – Sheriff Barnum

The Quick and the Dead (1995) – Ace Hanlon

Boulevard (1995) – McClaren

Color of Night (1994) – Buck

No Escape (1994) – Father

Spitfire (1994) – Richard Charles

Hard Target (1993) – Fouchon

Knights (1993) – Job

Man's Best Friend (1993) – Dr Jarret

The Outfit (1993) – Dutch Schultz

Super Mario Bros. (1993) – The King

Alien 3 (1992) – Bishop II

Delta Heat (1992) – Jackson Rivers

Excessive Force (1992) – Devlin

Jennifer Eight (1992) – Freddy Ross

Reason for Living: The Jill Ireland Story (1991)
– Charles Bronson

Stone Cold (1991) – Chains

The Pit and The Pendulum (1990) – Torquemada

Johnny Handsome (1989) – Rafe Garrett

Survival Quest (1989) – Hank

Deadly Intent (1988) – Raymond

Hit List (1988) – Chris Caleek

Pumpkinhead (1988) – Ed Harley

Near Dark (1987) – Jesse
Aliens (1986) – Bishop
Choke Canyon (1986) – Brook Alastair
Jagged Edge (1985) – Frank Martin
Savage Dawn (1985) – Stryker
Streets of Justice (1985) – District Attorney Jerry Logan
The Terminator (1984) – Vukovich
The Right Stuff (1983) – Wally Schirra
Piranha II: The Spawning (1981) – Steve Kimbrough
The Visitor (1979) – Raymond
Damien: Omen II (1978) – Sergeant Neff
Close Encounters of the Third Kind (1977) – Robert
Dog Day Afternoon (1975) – Murphy

CASE FILE: 'Wide Open'

CASE SYNOPSIS:

A series of risky murders leaves Frank and the Group chasing down a killer with a thing for high-tech security systems, gory murders – and no apparent motive! It's Catherine, however, who has the toughest job. The killer's youngest victim isn't dead. The girl, emotionally spent after witnessing the brutal murders of her parents, is also the only witness to his crimes and it's a toss up between the police and the killer as to who wants her most.

KEY CITATION:

'He left the child alive for a reason.
He signed the name "John Alworth" for
a reason. We'll catch him if we can
find out what that reason is.'

FRANK BLACK

VITAL STATISTICS:

Original US Airdate:	01/03/97
Production Number:	4C08
Written by:	Charles Holland
Directed by:	Jim Charleston

Guest Cast:

Pablo Coffey	Cutter
Stephen James	Detective Geibelhouse
Glynn Turman	James Glen
David Neale	John Highsmith
Sandra Ferens	Mary Kay Highsmith
Nevada Ash	Patricia Highsmith
Eileen Keney	Beverly Bunn
Carter Kagume	ICU Nurse
Roger R Cross	Officer Shaw
Ernie Prentice	Mr Marcelli
Colin McCarlie	Harry Marlowe
Mandy McKeen	Jane Marlowe
Cindy Lee	Riley Farnsworth

Death Toll:	3 females, 1 male, all axe-murdered

CASE HISTORY:

THE PEN IS AS REVEALING AS THE SWORD

'The signature is centrifugal, vertical lines, forward expansion. The strokes are forceful, measured, alternating cursive and print. This man's signature has probably been the same since he was old enough to sign it.'

JAMES GLEN, *on Unknown Subject's signature*

Considering the tiny sample James Glen worked with, just a few signatures scrawled in realtors' guest books, his ability to describe the suspect appears to rival even Frank Black's near-psychic ability to 'get inside the killer's mind'.

From just a few lines, he came up with ' … the signer is deliberate. He has focus, but that is to contain his rage, his anger, that he can be explosive, prone to violent outbursts.' In retrospect, his straightforward delivery probably told his fellow law enforcement officers a lot *more* than Frank's most enigmatic utterances.

So, without the assistance of psychic intervention and disjointed visions, how does graphology work? How does a graphologist, a handwriting analyst, pick apart the lines, dots and dashes to reveal human personality?

Well, not all graphologists do. Many are strictly Questioned Document Examiners. The QDE helps determine the age of documents, whether the document has been altered in any way, if signatures match or are more likely to have been forged. In conjunction with specialized chemists, they may analyze the type of ink, paper, impression methods, and perform chemical studies, anything that helps identify a particular sample. With the introduction of scanners, high-definition photocopiers, and graphic software, computer technicians became important members of the Suspect Document team.

A variety of so-called 'soft science' experts, ranging from criminal psychologists to theoretical linguists may also be attached to a unit studying the written messages of suspects. The Unabomber was identified as much by his choice of phrase, his grammar and syntax, the actual content of his messages, and the medium he employed to carry that message, as the technical details of the bombs he made. In *Millennium*'s second episode, 'Gehenna', audiences watch as the Group's Elder Statesman, Mike Atkins, compares the content of the victim's letter, including the type and number of verbs and use of the first person, with what might be expected of a cult inductee.

Document analysis, then, can encompass a number of disciplines but, while new technologies continue to open up new avenues of investigation, handwriting analysis is perhaps the oldest of the areas of inquiry and, in fact, shares some of the aspects of 'profiling' as practiced by law enforcement officers.

Like psychological profiling, handwriting-personality analysis grew out of a history of observation. Members of the FBI's Behavioral Science Unit spent literally thousands of man-hours interviewing serial murderers and rapists then matching what they knew of the crimes and crime scenes with the characteristics of criminals. Over time, criminal 'types' were identified by quantifiable characteristics, allowing experienced investigators to begin matching 'type' of criminal to particular factors at crime scenes with increasing accuracy and insight. In a similar way, handwriting analysts began noting similarities between personality types and their style of writing.

Anyone who's ever tried to forge a note to cut class realizes how difficult it is to not only match the strokes of their parent, but to eliminate the characteristics that make their own writing distinctive. Writing, which translates ideas and perceptions into concrete words, which are in turn formed of strokes of pen against paper, which in their turn are likely to be mere approximations of how the writer's mental eye first imagined the final written word would appear, is an intensely personal activity. Some of the most successful forgers claimed their best work appeared when they 'adopted the character of the writer'. That sounds suspiciously like Frank's technique for understanding serial criminals, doesn't it?

Handwriting, which extends back several thousand years, has come under close scrutiny for nearly as long. In Rome, where a man's signature had the force of law behind it if that man held public office, detailed descriptions of a man's style of writing weren't unusual. Caesar Augustus' was described by Deutonius Tranquillus in some detail, including: 'He does not separate his words, nor does he carry over to the next line any excess letters; instead, he places them under the final word and ties them to it with a stroke.'

However, while careful observers could make general comments on Augustus' style, they would also quickly realize that, even when they knew they were looking at work by the same man, there would be variations in the script. Just as no two crime scenes are ever identical, even when the crime is commited by the same criminal, no two signatures are indentical.

What graphology looks at are general traits that can be compared across samples. For example, while studying the signatures of thieves in the Paris police records back in the 1870s, a French investigator, Abbe Jean-Hippolyte Michon noticed that 30 to 40 per cent of those incarcerated didn't quite close the bottom of the circle in letters like 'o', 'd', or 'a'. What connection there might be between the bottoms of letters and a disregard for the ownership of property isn't known, may never be known, but it certainly exists. In his 30 years of comparing written language, Michon found the same trait among less than one per cent of the general populace. He wasn't all that surprised when several of those general citizens who didn't close their 'o' eventually were convicted of theft.

In the hundred years since Michon published a major volume of his observations, others have taken up the study and added their own clues and interpretations. In some countries, graphology was accepted as a science, much as profiling or criminal psychology. Other jurisdictions remained more dubious about the technique with regard to personality identification, but were quick to accept that graphology could address, through demonstrable changes in writing technique, the changing 'mental state' of a subject. Stress, drug or alcohol use, the onset of mental illnesses both organic and psychological, and transitory mood swings were certainly reflected in a subject's handwriting. In 1986, a Coroner's Court accepted graphological evidence as they attempted to determine if the death of a 19-year-old woman was suicide. With samples taken from her diary, a graphologist determined that, far from the depressed state one might expect to find in a suicide, the young woman was enjoying a period of high self-confidence and general satisfaction. When the finding was returned, the police weren't quite ready to write off the girl's death as an accident. She'd 'fallen' over a restraining fence some four feet high and down the face of a cliff. Further investigation revealed a former lover as her murderer.

Condensing the entire field of graphology in this constrained space is clearly impossible, but, if you'd like to attempt some general analysis of your own, or a friend's, handwriting, there are some characteristics you might look for. An expert, with years of experience in weighing the impact of one trait on another, would obviously return more detailed and accurate results but, for fun alone, get out a piece of letter-sized, *unlined* paper and write. Write anything you like, but write as much as you can. Your writing will become more natural as you proceed and forget you'll be 'analyzing' it later. If you're too self-conscious, find something you wrote earlier and just sign the bottom before proceeding to fill in your analysis chart.

HANDWRITING ANALYSIS WORKSHEET

When examining your writing sample, it may be handy to have a ruler and a protractor handy.

Remember, look for trends. If *most* of your 'i' letters have happy-face dots over them, but a few are strokes, go with the majority. Individuals are multi-faceted and the occasional inclusive of more than one type of trait is perfectly normal variation.

1 Look at your margins: the white space to either side of what you've written.

- [ ] Is the left margin more narrow than average (less than an inch)?
- [ ] Is the left margin wider than average (more than an inch-and-a half)?
- [ ] Is the right margin more narrow than average?
- [ ] Is the right margin wider than average?
- [ ] Are both side margins more narrow than average?
- [ ] Are both side margins wider than average?
- [ ] Do the margins slant to the left or right?
- [ ] Are the margins even?

2 How fast do you write?

- [ ] Swiftly
- [ ] Slowly
- [ ] Mixed speeds

3 What size is your writing?

- [ ] Huge overall (More than an inch tall)
- [ ] Large overall (Approaching an inch tall)
- [ ] Small overall (Approaching a quarter of an inch tall)
- [ ] Tiny overall (Less than a quarter of an inch tall)

4 How far apart are the lines of writing?

- [ ] Crowded (Parts of one actually touch another)
- [ ] Widely spaced (An inch between lines)

5 How far apart are the individual words?

- [ ] Words tend to run together
- [ ] Large white spaces between words (Half inch or more)
- [ ] Varied spaces (Some run together, some far apart)

CONTINUED

6   Given a choice, which type of pen/pencil/marker do you prefer to use?

☐ Very fine tip
☐ Fine tip
☐ Regular tip
☐ Heavier felt tip
☐ Very heavy tip

7   Slide a piece of lined paper under your work and determine which way your lines of writing slant.

☐ Wobbly. Runs through, over and under a straight line
☐ Slightly upward. Runs up through another line on the lined paper
☐ Steeply upward. Runs up through two or more lines of lined paper
☐ Slightly downward. Runs down through one line on the lined paper
☐ Steeply downward. Runs down through several lines of lined paper

8   Which way do your letters slant?

☐ Slightly forward, the average letter slope
☐ Steeply forward, 45 degrees or less of forward slope
☐ No slant, straight up and down
☐ Backward slant
☐ Steeply backward, 45 degrees or less of backward slope

NOTE: Omit altogether if the subject is left-handed.

9   How large are your letters? Look only at the lower-case letters of your sample.

☐ Tiny. Less than a quarter of an inch high
☐ Small. Less than a half an inch high
☐ Large. About an inch high
☐ Huge. Consistently more than an inch high
☐ Varied. Ranges from half an inch to more than an inch within one word
☐ Shrinking. Starts large and tapers off to small within one word
☐ Enlarging. Starts small and expands to large within one word
☐ Stroking. Words taper into straight lines with no visible letters

CONTINUED

10 Check your letter zones. An ascender is the part of a letter that extends upward, like the stroke of a 'b' or 'd' that extends above the circular section. A descender is the part that falls below the line of writing, like the stroke of a 'p' or a 'y'. The mid-zone of a letter is the part that sits on the line of writing, like the circles in 'p' or 'b'. All of an 'a' is normally in the mid-zone region.

- ☐ Dominant ascenders. The upward strokes are exaggerated
- ☐ Dominant descenders. The downward strokes are exaggerated
- ☐ Dominant mid-zone. Virtually no ascenders or descenders
- ☐ Equal zones. Ascenders, descenders, and mid-zone are equal size

11 Look at the 'i' in your sample. See if they match these descriptions. Remember, there may be some variation between your letters. If one description dominates, use that. If there are fairly equal numbers of several descriptions, include them all.

- ☐ Dot-less 'i'. No dot above the letter at all
- ☐ Barely-there dot. Tough to pick out
- ☐ Blob-dot. A huge, often messy, dot
- ☐ Circle dot. Usually unfilled circle. If filled-in, call it a blob dot
- ☐ Directly above. Is the dot vertically above the tip of the 'i'?
- ☐ High dot. At the level of a tall ascender
- ☐ High and right. At the level of a tall ascender but 'leading' the 'i'
- ☐ Low dot. Barely separated from the 'i'. May even be below the tip of the 'i'
- ☐ Low and right. Like a low dot, but 'in front' of the 'i'
- ☐ Low and left. This dot follows along 'behind' the 'i'
- ☐ Dash-dot. Instead of a point, this dot is a stroke of the pen
- ☐ Claret-dot. Forms a little 'tent' over the 'i'
- ☐ Reversed claret-dot. Looks like a little frown over the 'i'

12 Compare the signature to the main body of the text.

- ☐ Signature a little larger than text
- ☐ Similar in size to the text
- ☐ Smaller in comparison to the text
- ☐ Huge, ornate. Much larger than the writing in the text, often features an elaborate flourish

Now, see what your answers reveal!

MARGINS

Narrow left margin:	Tends to the practical instead of artistic.
Wide left margin:	Tends to the artistic, open-minded.
Narrow right margin:	A social person, realistic.
Wide right margin:	Tad self-conscious, maybe shy or less realistic.
Crowded both sides:	Either busy or stingy.
Wide on both sides:	Tends to prefer their own company, be artistic and sensitive, not a group leader.
Mixed margins:	If left slants to the left, the person is ambiguous. Tends to the extravagant, but may curb that tendency at the last minute. If left slants to the right, the reverse is true. Subject may try very hard to stick to a budget, for example, but get that new pair of sneakers anyway.
Regular, even:	A person of discrimination.

SPEED

Swift:	Busy, or anxious.
Slow:	Attentive to detail, or hesitant.
Varied:	Suggests inner disagreements.

SIZE

Huge overall:	Someone who attempts to call attention, even if undeserved, to themselves. May also be a bully given the opportunity.
Large overall:	A confident, self-assured person who doesn't draw undue attention. Likes to stand out in a group, but in a very natural way.
Small overall:	Meticulous attention to detail, strong power of concentration, quiet.
Tiny overall:	Intelligent, but introverted. May not be a good mixer, may be 'emotionally stingy'.

LINE SPACING

Crowded:	Quiet, not extravagant with money or emotion. May not be open to new ideas.
Widely spaced:	Usually out-going, a lover of the arts, often musically inclined. Enjoys being generous.

WORD SPACING

Tightly spaced:	May be 'uptight'. Shy, wary, but also discreet and considerate.
Wide scrawl:	Likely to be a dare-devil, extroverted, and generous – often to a fault.
Varied spaces:	Flighty, disorganized, the stereotypical 'nutty professor'.

SCRIPT THICKNESS

Very fine tip:	Generally shy, modest, sensitive, generous. Not a group leader.
Fine tip:	Jackie O's favorite type, refined, retiring, but not shy, quietly self-assured.
Regular tip:	A well-balanced person.
Heavier felt tip:	A doer. Confident, self-assured, out-going, extroverted, physical.
Very heavy tip:	More exaggerated version of the Heavier Felt Tip, a real 'Alpha' personality.

LINE SLANT

Wobbly:	Tendency to carelessness, moodiness and sloppiness.
Slightly upward:	Happy-go-lucky, optimistic, satisfied.
Steeply upward:	Likely to be unrealistic, ambitious.
Slightly downward:	Typical of the 'half-empty' type. No specific complaints, just general depression.
Steeply downward:	Abnormally depressed, with or without cause.

LETTER SLANT

Slightly forward:	The average letter slope.
Steeply forward:	Emotional, possibly artistic, sensitive to opinion, somewhat needy emotionally.

No slant:	Outwardly unemotional, clear thinker, something of a loner in the self-reliant sense, not a group person. More likely to favor the sciences than the arts.
Backward slant:	The true loner, introverted, perfectly average slant for the developing teen.
Steeply backward:	Unusual degree of separation from self and society, singular lack of close friends or even close acquaintances.

LETTER SIZE – LOWER-CASE LETTERS

Tiny:	A creative and open-minded thinker, unconcerned about outside opinion or public image.
Small:	Also creative, but impulsive … often too impulsive.
Large:	Emotionally temperamental, but generous with time and resources, generally out-going, self-assured.
Huge:	Just too, too much. May be tacky. Loud. Given to acting abruptly and without thought.
Varied:	Shrewd.
Shrinking:	Aware of the 'main chance'. Likely to get the better of peers.
Enlarging:	An expansive personality, generous, if not always wise.
Stroking:	Busy, or moody.

LETTER ZONES

| Dominant ascenders: | The original day-dream believer. Upbeat and optimistic, but not particularly realistic. |
| Dominant descenders: | Strong physical aspects, either sexual or athletic, or both. |

| Dominant mid-zone: | Grounded individual, not brilliant or artistic, but loaded with common sense. |
| Equal zones: | The well-rounded person who is comfortable with themselves and, consequently, with others. |

SPECIFIC LETTERS

Dot-less 'i':	Fails to follow through on plans.
Barely-there dot:	Withdrawn, retiring, non-mixer.
Blob-dot:	Tendency to dominate, perhaps to the point of cruelty.
Circle dot:	Likes to be the center of attention, tends towards the 'artsy'.
Directly above:	Stays the course, responsible.
High dot:	Creative.
High and right:	Impulsive, 'glass half-full' type.
Low dot:	Attentive to detail.
Low right:	Like a raccoon, curious.
Low left:	The ultimate procrastinator, but careful.
Dash-dot:	Vibrant, active, sometimes just too busy.
Claret dot:	The scientific mind, keen, intelligent, creative if not artistic.
Reverse claret:	Witty, great sense of humor.

THE SIGNATURE CLUES – SIZE

Somewhat larger:	A strong sense of self.
Similar:	Contented, unlikely to dissemble.
Smaller:	Unsatisfied with the self, regardless of actual real worth.
Huge, ornate:	Portrays a vivacious, out-going personality, which may be a front.

NOTEBOOK:

Changes In The Wings

As this episode went to air, a flurry of *Millennium* news made the rounds, not all of it positive.

In Vancouver, Canada, where both *Millennium* and *The X-Files* are filmed, movements intended to curb violence on TV targeted *Poltergeist: The Legacy* and *Millennium* for their special attention. A concerted letter-writing campaign hit high gear with The Coalition of Responsible Television focusing on the advertisers buying space on the two shows.

At the same time, North Vancouver councillor Ernie Crist put it to his colleagues in government that it was somewhat hypocritical to allocate thousands of dollars promoting anti-violence campaigns while, at the same time, allowing violent programs to use government buildings, facilities and recreation areas for their filming needs.

Then, the following week, *Millennium*'s Nielsen numbers sank to a disappointing 6.8, the worst results to date for a first run episode.

BLETCH, FRANK AND CATHERINE WATCH OVER YOUNG NEVADA ASH WHO TURNS IN AN ENCHANTING PERFORMANCE AS PATRICIA HIGHSMITH

TESTIMONY TRIVIA 9

These people, places and events should stand out in your mind.
Take one point for each correct answer.

QUESTIONS

1   What did Giebelhouse suggest could easily replace a $5000 security system?
2   Where did Frank find Patricia Highsmith?
3   Who did Bletch jokingly suggest as the subject of an APB?
4   What do Travis Bickle and Rudyard Holmbast have in common?
5   What does Jordan give Patricia?

These may prove more of a brain strain. Take two points each accurate recall.

6   To which realty agency did the Killer send his video tape?
7   What symbol did Frank find under a doormat?
8   In which high-security community did Frank and Bletch, with the help of a dog, apprehend the Killer?
9   Where did Frank, Bletcher, and several more cops hide during their stakeout?
10 What does Bletcher offer to a guard dog?

Within two weeks, Fox Entertainment President Peter Roth was talking 'new characters', 'cosmic conspiracy', and expanding storylines. Other reports, better termed brush-fire rumors, and quickly squashed, hinted at a female partner for Frank Black. More reliable sources, however, agreed that a partner of some type had been discussed, and was still an open question. More official statements followed quickly, indicating that perhaps Carter and company, in trying to distance *Millennium* from *The X-Files*, had created an unworkable environment for the new series.

So, as the February Sweeps Week approached, and as networks began deciding which shows would be renewed, 'new directions' were announced for *Millennium*. Viewers could expect to see a turn back towards the extraordinary, hints dropped earlier that perhaps Black's daughter also saw things 'differently' would be developed, and stronger efforts would be made to flesh out Megan Gallagher's role.

Millennium fans, after watching 'The Well-Worn Lock' and 'Wide Open', couldn't help thinking that at least one of those items, Catherine Black's character, was coming along just fine without any 're-tooling'.

INCIDENTAL:

Patricia Highsmith, the name of the child in this episode, is also the name of one of Hitchcock's favorite mystery writers. He turned one of her novels, *Strangers on a Train*, into a film and cast his daughter as one of the main characters.

'I think he's a character with tremendous sex appeal.'

CHRIS CARTER on Frank Black

Brittany Tiplady, the adorable ray of sunshine on the *Millennium* set, isn't allowed to watch an entire episode of her own show. Instead, she gets an edited version featuring her own scenes – every little actress's dream!

CASE FILE: 'Weeds'

CASE SYNOPSIS:

Frank's profiling skills quickly implicate a resident of a high-class, gated community in the kidnapping and grizzly murder of his neighbors' kids – a view the rest of the citizens simply can't accept. The killer's intimate knowledge of the teens's parents, however, soon provides evidence even this close-knit neighborhood can't ignore, along with a home-grown motive.

KEY CITATION:

'The kidnapper sees himself as
a holy figure, a purifier. He makes
the impure ingest his blood so that
they can be cleansed.'

FRANK BLACK

VITAL STATISTICS:

Original US Airdate:	01/24/97
Production Number:	4C09
Written by:	Frank Spotnitz
Directed by:	Michael Pattinson

Guest Cast:

CCH Pounder	Cheryl Andrews
Don Mackay	Jack Meredith
Ryan Cultrona	Sheriff Paul Gerlach
Josh Clark	Edward Petey
Karen Kruper	Mrs Petey
A J Buckley	Josh
Michael Tomlinson	Mr Comstock
Joy Rinaldi	Mrs Comstock
Terry David Mulligan	Mr Birckenbuehl
Jade Pawluk	Charlie Birckenbuehl
Betty Phillips	Abby
Andrew Johnston	The Coroner
Brian Taylor	Coach Burke
Paul Batten	The Priest
Fred Henderson	The Lawyer
Rick Ravanello	The Cop

Death Toll:	1 male, by suicide
	1 boy, bled to death

CASE HISTORY:

DO YOU SEE
WHAT I SEE? From the beginning, audiences have been asking how Frank Black does whatever it is he does. Is he psychic? Are profilers some special breed of

law enforcement officer with brains that, like the killers they track, operate 'differently' from the rest of us?   So differently that we can never hope to gain even a glim-mer of their vision? Or, are they so good at picking up the subliminal hints around them that a totally natural ability   to see clues combines with their personal and professional experience, enabling them to return results that just seem 'supernat-ural'? And, of course, in the case of a fictional   scenario like *Millennium*, there's always a second ques-tion: 'Just how close to reality is a character like Frank Black'?

According to Dean Cant, a former behavioral scientist in the Los Angeles area, and Penda MacIntyre, his current business partner and a sixteen-year profiling veteran from the east coast, it's 'surprisingly accurate'.

From their cramped quarters in Penda's half of their pair of home offices, a setup eerily reminiscent of The Yellow House's basement – with the exception that Penda MacIn-tyre has reached the wallboard and plaster stage – the two former agents eye a monitor airing the latest episode of *Millennium*, 'Weeds'. A stack of videos from earlier shows sits next to the remains of a jumbo popcorn. As CCH Pounder, Group member Cheryl Andrews in the *Millennium* uni-verse, hooks a blood-filled football out from under a victim's bed, Dean chuckles, 'With the exception of stuff like that.' Turning serious, he adds, 'Not that weird stuff doesn't get brought to crime scenes – not at all. Just a couple of months ago, we consulted on a case where the criminal brought a papier mâché doll to deliberately leave at the scene. It's just highly unlikely that the investigators at the scene would miss a football that sloshed when they moved it, or was of an inappropriate weight for its size or composi-tion.'

Penda nods slowly, rewinds, and watches Frank's next 'vision'. 'I think this thing that he does falls into the same boat. From a technical point of view, he asks all the right questions, makes all the right comments. He acts "right".'

'Exactly,' Dean agrees. 'Good writing, good character research here. Remembering that this *is* television, where the audience has a limited number of ways of 'getting into' this Frank Black's head—'

'Books are easier.' His partner adds quickly, 'You don't have to *show* it visually. In books, you can drop clues to the investigator's thought processes. On TV, you've got to *show* something – otherwise, the actor just stares deeply into the camera, or something equally boring, everytime he thinks.'

'These "visions" don't suggest anything "psychic" to me,' Dean continues. 'Crime scene evidence is much more compelling than most laymen realize. There are people who, for example, can walk through a crime scene and tell you who went where, how much they struggled on the way, and the exact physical point where they simply gave up or were overcome – just from the blood splatters! Me, I have to meticulously examine every drop, determine its direction and distance of fall fairly scientifically, and, *slowly* build up an image of the action.

'When I was working a murder-suicide in San Francisco many years ago, one of the detectives who'd taken me out to the scene just stopped at a spot midway down a back hallway. He glanced from the floor to the door and mumbled, "Poor kid, almost made it too." He knew from the pattern that the victim had actually gotten away from her attacker at some point, run down this hall, been recaptured there and, after a terrific struggle, died there. Nothing psychic going on, just the natural reconstruction of events that the technicians would later confirm with references to specific blood drops. I'm sure, in that detective's mind, he wasn't just categorizing blood droplets. He was adding her face, the sounds of her screams, the terror we know accompanies such an attack, building a picture that, while not an exact duplication of each moment, certainly, gave the *sense* of events in that house on that night.'

Leaning across and rewinding the tape again, MacIntyre points at some of the swiftly moving images. 'There's a lot of perfectly legitimate work going on here. Like this scene where Black attends the victim's funeral. Happens all the time, for just the reasons he states.' She stops and lets the tape run forward.

Lance Henriksen's deep voice fills the small space.

'The killer is between 35 and 45 years old, drives a late-model car, probably a mini-van or sport utility vehicle. I believe his parents were divorced when he was a child. If he's married, his wife doesn't know anything about the crimes he's committing.'

'*This* is what most people think of when they hear about criminal profiles. This type of detailed description. As Black later admits he was just fishing, we don't know how seriously this 'profile' was meant to be taken. However, even when investigators are chumming, they'll usually come across straight on a profile. In that other episode ['Dead Letters'], they did the thing with the misspelled word, to try and drag him out before he was ready. That's a good proactive plan with the meticulous killer, almost identical to what happens in this scene when he tells the killer he thinks he's insane. And, for a profile in this area, it was as good an assessment of the facts as any.'

Dean begins ticking off points on his fingers. 'Look at the community. Statistically, we know that most killers stay within their ethnic group. Whites kill whites, blacks kill blacks, yadda, yadda, yadda. Well, there weren't a whole lot of ethnic groups at that community meeting, were there? So, if a killer comes from within the community, the killer is going to appear to be like everyone else—'

'With statistical variation.' Penda grins. 'First-year course work, but true.'

'Statistics are as big a part of profiling as intuition, though, the really good investigators seem to be both knowledgeable and empathic. They can look at evidence and work backwards through all the theory, but still recognize the … the personality at work in the scene.'

Turning off the tape altogether, the partners become even more serious. 'It's important,' Dean begins, 'To understand the man-hours that have gone into the statistics. Some number-crunching is relatively meaningless but, if someone tells me they've got an organized crime scene, like the ones in this episode, I can, because hundreds of investigators have shared their experience and knowledge before me, tell you some pretty specific things about that killer.'

'He – and it will likely be a he,' Penda grins, 'there are women serial killers, but, they don't do this kind of crime. More stats. Anyway, *he* will be of at least average intelligence, probably, as in this case, a professional of some type, college or university educated. He'll look like all his neighbors, be sociable, probably married or, if not married single by choice, root for the local sports teams, all that stuff. There's a good chance he'll follow his own press. He'll be older, mature socially, sexually, psychologically. He won't panic under questioning. He'll move the body but, when he does dispose of it, it'll be to some purpose. He won't leave a lot of evidence for you, unless he has something to say. His actions are planned, his victims thought out ahead of time. He controls the victim, the scene, everything he can. It's perfectly consistent to find restraints still tied around the bodies of his victims.'

Dean nods. 'There will be variation, but you will never find a highly organized, staged scene, from an eighteen-year-old kid who suddenly gets pissed with his girlfriend and

TESTIMONY TRIVIA 10

1   Which birthday did Josh celebrate the day of his abduction?
2   Name the community the killer chose to terrorize.
3   What did Kirk Orlando's father find in his mailbox?
4   What odd weapon did the killer use to subdue his victims?
5   How does Frank attempt to force the killer's hand?
6   What was written across the Comstocks' bed?
7   Which sci-fi series did Charlie Birchenbuehl watch before being kidnapped?
8   What was delivered to the Merediths' house?
9   What, besides water and dead fish, was in Charlie's fishtank?
10 Who owned the football under the bed?

whacks her on the head with the closest available object. The two are incompatible.'

Penda nods towards the stack of tapes, then taps 'Dead Letters' briefly. 'Professionally speaking, this is my favorite, though "Weeds" is a close second. "Dead Letters" illustrates the difficulties of the job – half the people I've worked with

VIEWERS CAN'T HELP WONDERING WHEN FRANK WILL FIND TIME TO PUT WALLS AROUND HIS OFFICE

are divorced, alienated from their families ... plain miserable, burnt out. But, it's a good example of what behavioral science brings to an investigation. What we do isn't a real science, but, it's not "art" either. I think of it as craft. Writers learn the basics of grammar, spelling, format like the rest of us, but there's no school that hands out a diploma that says so-and-so is now a qualified writer. Experience, effort and at least a hint of inspiration make words live, the grammar helps gets the words to readers in forms they understand. Profiling is like that. You see enough crime scenes, you study enough case histories, you start to make associations that aren't taught in the classroom – though those instructors certainly try to twist your head around to the right perspective – and you make these unconscious assumptions. Some of it probably is that intangible ... instinct, most of it is hard work, study, experience, and more study.'

Dean stacks the tapes neatly. 'I wouldn't have minded having a guy like this on our side from time to time, but, ya know what? Even knowing what I know, I think I'd still have found Frank Black a little ... scary.'

NOTEBOOK:

The Many Meanings of Blood

Since humanity's earliest memories, blood has simultaneously fascinated and repulsed us. Even modern children respond vehemently to it. There are, after all, only two possible reactions to a gashed knee or elbow: run screaming for the nearest parent, the cut held as far from the rest of the body as possible, or stare in wonder at the red liquid welling up until a finger smears it about.

Some early tribes believed blood was a contaminant. Menstruating women were ostracized from the group. Dwellings were erected far from known battlefields. Animals were bled before being brought back for community consumption. The blood of an enemy, gathered and burnt, gave you the power of death over that individual.

A considerably larger number of cultures, however, revered blood, associating it with the soul, with life, with the sun, with whatever positive forces affected them.

The killer in 'Weeds' followed ancient European, African and Eastern traditions. Even before Christian priests enjoined their followers to 'Take this wine and drink it in remembrance of me. It is my Blood, shed for thee' other cultures regarded blood as a purificant, not only for the soul, but for the body.

In Greece, blood, either soaked into flat breads or mixed with wine, was standard fare for the sick. Sprinkled in the bottom of new graves, it gave new life to the spirit passing into the next world. Roman seers, before sorcery became a dangerous occupation for political reasons, smeared blood over their faces and hands to ensure their protection from evil spirits as they sought their augeries. A seasonal bath of blood was proof against the worst diseases of the time.

More figurative blood baths supplied several medieval madmen, and madwomen, with the gallons of water required for their baths. The Countess de Medici was so convinced her bloody ablutions kept her young and beautiful that she frequently sacrificed a serving girl or two over her deep tub.

In a turnaround from the *Millennium* example, modern madman William Goeth killed and drank his victims' blood in an effort to purify himself, to cast out the 'voices' telling him to kill in the first place. Talk about your self-fulfilling prophecies!

A N S W E R S

1 His 16th
2 Vista Verde Estates
3 'Eight dollars worth of confetti'
4 A cattle prod
5 By goading him, by publically calling him 'insane'
6 '331' – in blood
7 *Land of the Giants*
8 A paint chip. Give yourself an extra point if you remember the color number was 528, and a third point if you remember the color name was Forest Green, found on 'late-model ML750 mini-vans'.
9 Scotch
10 Carl Burke, the coach's dead son

YOUR SCORE:

INCIDENTALS:

Like producer Chris Carter, Lance Henriksen makes pottery in his spare time.

☐

A typical shooting day on *Millennium* runs anywhere from twelve to sixteen hours, rain or shine. An extra working on the program characterized the difference between working in Vancouver and working in LA rather simply. 'In LA, you stand around under umbrellas to protect yourself from the sun. Up here, umbrellas actually have to be waterproof!'

☐

The slow-fade in at the beginning of each scene in *Millennium* is intended to mimic the development of a photograph, a subtle reminder of the Polaroid Stalker and his mail-in campaign.

☐

Asked what he thought of the Internet response to the show, Carter replied, 'Harsh.'

'The Wild And The Innocent

CASE SYNOPSIS:

When Frank Black joins a manhunt dedicated to tracking cop killer, Jake Waterman, a man already high on Frank's personal agenda for three prior murders, Frank has no intention of letting the man slip through his fingers a second time. However, despite some scanty forensic evidence and considerable police pressure, his instincts lead him, instead, to a heartbroken young mother and her tarnished knight-in-shining-armour – and to a series of crime scenes that document all too clearly the couple's escalating violence.

TEN-THIRTEEN'S ATTENTION TO ALL THE ANGLES, BOTH PLOT AND CINEMATOGRAPHIC, CREATES UNIQUE IMAGES FOR THEIR AUDIENCES

KEY CITATION:

'There's a young woman involved.
I believe she's with the killer,
but an innocent.'

FRANK BLACK

VITAL STATISTICS:

Original US Airdate:	01/10/97
Production Number:	4C10
Written by:	Jorge Zamacona
Directed by:	Thomas Wright

Guest Cast:

Terry O'Quinn	Peter Watts
Heather McComb	Maddie Haskell
Jeffery Donovan	Billy Webber
John Pyper-Ferguson	Jim Gilroy
Michael Hogan	Captain Bigelow
Jim Swansburg	Sam Travis
Renee Michelle	Adeline Travis
Gina Chiarelli	Killean Marie Haskell
Jim Poyner	Mr Nesmith
Mary Black	Mrs Nesmith

Death Toll:	1 lawyer, shot off-screen
	1 couple, shot on-screen

CASE HISTORY:

THE COUPLES WHO DO EVERYTHING TOGETHER

When *Natural Born Killers* swept through theatres, it certainly piqued the public's interest in killer couples, but it took *Millennium* to put a new spin on the guy meets girl, girl gets gun, guy and girl get everyone plot line.

The typical plot line is best illustrated by real-life couple David and Catherine Birnie who terrorized, raped and murdered four women in four weeks.

The two were childhood acquaintances and teenaged lovers, who, after bungling their first conjoint criminal efforts as burglars, went their separate ways. Catherine married and began raising five children. David also married, but due to the exhorbitant amount of time he spent in mental institutions, not to mention his excessively demanding sexual appetites, the relationship floundered. When the two met again, Catherine dumped husband, home and family to pair up with her old lover.

For the first year or so, things seeemed relatively normal. Then, when a young woman came to the door enquiring about some car tires David advertized in the For Sale columns, Mary Neilson became the couple's first victim. What triggered it remains unknown, but, with Catherine holding a knife to Mary's throat, David savagely raped the twenty-two-year-old. Suddenly, the Birnies had an hysterical woman on their hands, one they couldn't allow out of their home if they were to avoid arrest for the rape. Like so many others who realize their impetuous acts have robbed them of the opportunity to just walk away, or to simply dump the victim some distance away, the Birnies quickly decided it was in their own best interest to kill her. However, when they reached their chosen dump site, a remote area in Glen Eagle National Park, David Birnie raped Mary again before

Catherine joined the act to strangle and disfigure her before tossing her into a depression hardly worthy of the term 'grave'.

In a matter of hours, Catherine and David had discovered a whole new facet of their relationship, something they shared in addition to their own sexual antics. What might have happened had either partner shown shock or remorse is a good, if unanswerable, question. What *did* happen was a sudden escalation to violence that neither David nor Catherine had ever individually exhibited before.

The very next week, the couple began hunting. Victim number two, a fifteen-year-old they'd spotted hitch-hiking, thought herself safe enough accepting a ride from a middle-aged couple. Imagine the young woman's horror when Catherine helped her husband subdue the girl, then confine her in their house where she was kept as a sex slave to David's voracious appetites. Once again, it was Catherine who eventually strangled the girl before she and David found their next victim. Victim number three was no stranger to the Birnies, but that didn't protect her. Noelene Patterson died with David's hands clutching her throat. After three days of brutal sexual assaults, he lost interest in her. Some speculate that, of the two, Catherine incited the worst rounds of violence. Though David killed Noelene, he did it *after* the woman was heavily drugged. Their fourth victim died a mere two days after her abduction, but they were 48 of David Birnie's most violent hours. When the raped and battered woman ended up in Catherine's hands, Catherine didn't strangle her – she stabbed her repeatedly before leaving the body in the woods. The level of violence reached in just 34 days, by two previously petty crooks, shocked even hardened investigators.

What the cops discovered was the bizarre dynamics existing between so-called killer couples. Their solo counterparts, which make up more than 80 per cent of all serial criminals, may take years to escalate to similar levels of violence. Typical solo killers spend years teasing neighborhood pets, eventually killing one, catching houses on fire, working their way up to the 'main event'. Killer couples feed one another's fantasies, helping each other relive the excitement, condoning one another's activities by their participation. For them, the main event easily becomes their opening act. There's no knowing just how far the Birnies' depravity might have taken them. If not for the unexpected escape of their fifth victim, it might have been years before they became suspects, much less were caught. In that time, at the blazing pace they'd set for themselves, the Birnies might easily have racked up one of the highest kill rates in recorded criminal history.

Carol Bundy and Douglas Clark, half a world away from the Birnies' Australian hunting grounds, were, nonetheless, firmly in the race. They began with a bang – two of them actually – by abducting two step-sisters at the same time. Carol was the lure, enticing the girls into Clark's car. Once inside, he forced them to the floor of the vehicle, demanded oral sex by putting a gun to their heads, then shot them in the middle of the act. Once again, the escalation was swift. The next victims, after being treated to the same regime as the step-sisters, were decapitated. Clark liked to bring the heads, kept carefully frozen between events, into the bedroom with him. He also assaulted the women's dead bodies before dumping them. Like the Birnies', Bundy and Clark's quickly increasing violence was cut short by capture. After killing one friend who'd become suspicious, Carol Bundy, for no known reason, confessed all to another friend – who wasted no time getting the police involved.

While many aspects of the Birnies' case mirror those of the Bundy-Clark case, there remains a significant difference. Carol Bundy, unlike Catherine Birnie, wasn't the lead player. Though the vast majority of killer couples participate nearly equally in their joint depravities, cases like the one featured in 'The Wild and The Innocent', where one partner completely dominates the other, do arise.

Percy Campion and Diddi Michaels seemed a fairly ordinary couple, though visitors to their home had, from time to time, commented on the presence of a dog pillow by the side of their bed since neither of the pair owned a dog. Jokingly, Percy would explain that Diddi fell out of bed so often, he'd put the thick pillow there to break her fall. No one knew about the dog leash, the whip, and the electric training collar he kept in his bedside table. Nor did they realize that Diddi hadn't actually slept in her own bed since she'd moved into Campion's house two years ago. She'd been beaten on the bed, raped on it repeatedly, tied to it and cigarette-burned about her breasts and genitalia, but never, even once, had she slept on it.

When Midwight police eventually apprehended Campion and Michaels for the murder of six women and two men, Campion resolutely denied his guilt. Michaels, when asked if she'd participated in any of the killings, replied, 'I'm guilty. I'm guilty. Guilty.' She had no comment on Campion's participation.

Something about the scenario struck Det. Harold Bennton as more than odd. 'She's way past creepy,' he informed their commanding officer – right before asking that the department psychologist be asked to observe the remainder of the questioning. Michaels had already waived her right to an attorney, to silence, to anything that might slow down the signing of her brief confession but, impressed by an experienced officer's reluctance to close a case, the CO agreed and called in not only the requested psychologist, but more officers to finish the search of Campion's house.

It took officers a flat two hours and twelve minutes to return with scrapbooks, video tapes, and the animal training equipment. Three and a half hours later, an hysterical Diddi Michaels was turned over to Midwight's local emergency clinic. On being shown the photos of eight deceased youths, all of which featured Percy Campion, Diddi had simply closed her eyes and refused to speak. When shown the electric collar, her reaction shocked even the attending psychologist who later noted, 'Ms Michaels, having already determined there was little in the room to use as any sort of a weapon, threw herself against the window separating us from the visiting rooms next door.' Diddi wasn't looking for a weapon to turn on police. Instead, 'She dragged both wrists across the broken glass before attempting to slit her own throat.'

At the hospital, Diddi remained comatose for nearly three days, ample time for the staff to discover the multitude of injuries hidden under the pink tracksuit she'd been wearing when picked up. Forty-two burns, nineteen 'significant' lacerations, seven broken bones, including two serious breaks at the occipital area of her skull, and 'considerable scarring from unknown sources'.

The Diddi Michaels who calmly served coffee at her common-law husband's dinner parties was a sham. So was the woman one witness had seen during one of the abductions, the woman who'd sat in the driver's seat, leaning over the wheel, feigning illness until someone stopped and came close enough to discover Percy Campion hunched on the rear seat with a pistol pointed at them. To almost anyone passing, it would appear the victim got in the car to accompany a distressed young woman home.

In the months of intense therapy and investigation following Diddi Michaels's attempted suicide, the entire story gradually came to light. Diddi, who friends admitted was of a 'particularly meek' disposition prior to meeting Percy Campion, had participated in only one of the killings, the first. The victim, a young woman, had been tied to the bed before Diddi arrived home. Once she'd entered the room, Campion had locked the 'suped-up' training collar around Diddi's neck and pressed a knife into her hand before

TESTIMONY TRIVIA 11

1 What's scratched into the TV screen?
2 What does Frank find amid the tub scum?
3 Gilroy's blood type wasn't B−, what was it?
4 Name the Nesmiths' dog, the one who objected to Bobby's intrusion.
5 What did Jake Waterman use to kill his victims?
6 What was Angel's birthday?
7 What did Maddie and Bobby bring to the Travis house?
8 How many women did Waterman kill over a Labor Day weekend?
9 What did Jordan ask her parents for?
10 Where did Frank find Jim Gilroy, aka Jake Waterman?

repeatedly shocking her and ordering her to stab the other woman. Diddi Michaels has no recollection of how long this torture continued, when she lost track of that time, or whether she actually killed Cyndi Kazynski. She awoke sometime during the night, in her usual spot on the dog pillow, naked except for the collar, with Kazynski's icy body in her arms.

Percy Campion is serving eight consecutive life sentences. Diddi Michaels, at her own request, remains in an institute for the criminally insane.

Clearly, the fictional Maddie Haskel retained some freedom of choice when she chose to accompany her man on their road trip through hell, a choice she exercised after attaining her goal, but, finding a spot for her on the spectrum of killer couples shouldn't be easy for *Millennium*'s viewers. This program, which bills itself as a series of modern morality plays, a direct confrontation between good and evil, seems to delight in presenting its fans with ambiguous situations that leave viewers vascillating between sympathy and callous indifference.

NOTEBOOK:

Following The Electronic Trail

'We're running it through NCIC,' is a common refrain on *Millennium* – and just about every other program in the cop/mystery milieu. Hardly surprising considering it's one of the few nationwide criminal reporting systems and, by extension, one of the few ways to track criminals across state boundaries. Without it, there'd be few ways for even the Millennium Group to connect a spree killing up in Newport News with a cop-killing in the deep south.

Managed by the FBI, NCIC, the National Crime Information Center, maintains searchable databases on, among other things, outstanding arrest warrants like the one filed against Jake Waterman, unidentified persons, missing persons, criminal histories including fingerprint files and offense histories, and records of stolen properties, everything from license plates to boats. All 50 American states, as well as the federal agencies of the USA, Canada, and Puerto Rico have access to the system. Through its links to both Interpol and Canada's own databases, NCIC also tracks fugitives seeking to escape *into* the United States.

ANSWERS
1 'ANGEL'
2 Blood
3 A–
4 Lottie
5 Fishing line, 10 lb test line
6 14 July
7 Flowers
8 Three
9 A sister!
10 In the trunk of a submerged car
YOUR SCORE:

Somewhat ironically, the same database system also includes the files of missing children throughout the United States. Had Maddie Haskell's son ever been reported missing, his file would have eventually arrived at the Missing and Exploited Children National Center. This agency, though not part of the federal system at all, receives massive support from all levels of law enforcement. All missing children on its register are known to NCIC and, through the database, to the hundreds of thousands of police officers who work at street level.

Of the nearly one million children reported missing each year, over 60 per cent are recorded with NCIC in less than 24 hours.

The Missing and Exploited Children National Center also publishes statistics and photographs of missing children independently of other agencies. They know that while 5000 children will be snatched by strangers, *347,000* will be taken by friends and family members. On a more hopeful note, they also know that approximately one in seven of the photos they circulate will result in a child returned unharmed. It's their hope that, by working smarter, harder and faster, they'll reduce the number, currently something over 300, of cases where the child is found dead, becoming part of some criminal file in the NCIC system.

INCIDENTALS:

ACTRESS FILMOGRAPHY:
HEATHER MCCOMB

Although considerably younger than the regular cast of *Millennium*, Heather McComb brought a considerable amount of acting experience to her superb portrayal of Maddie Haskell.

Generation X (1996) – Jubilee
No One Would Tell (1996) – Nikki
Chicago Hope (1995) – Melissa Connel
The X-Files (1995) – Shannon Ausbury
Due South (1994) – Celine
Beethoven's 2nd (1993) – Michelle
Stay Tuned (1992) – Diane Knable
Kickboxer 2: The Road Back (1991) – Lisa
The Outsiders (1989) – Belinda Jenkins
New York Stories (1989) – Zoe

Just weeks after appearing on *Millennium*, Heather McComb was a featured performer on 'the other profiling show', *Profiler*, where she played Frances Malone, the troubled daughter of Violent Crimes Taskforce leader, Special Agent Bailey Malone.

CASE FILE: 'Loin Like A Hunting Flame'

CASE SYNOPSIS:

Sex, drugs and videotape combine in a sexual sadist's wild fantasies – until the dreams aren't enough, until the murderous fantasies become real. The hostility and gender bias of the lead investigator, a Det. Thomas, especially towards Millennium Group member Maureen Murphy, makes determining motive or uncovering the culprit all the more difficult.

KEY CITATION:

'He's moving towards the consummation of an act he is incapable of consummating. Not with his wife. Not with anyone.'

MAUREEN MURPHY

VITAL STATISTICS:

Original US Airdate:	01/31/97
Production Number:	4C11
Written by:	Ted Mann
Directed by:	David Nutter

Guest Cast:

Terry O'Quinn	Peter Watts
Harriet Sansom	Maureen Murphy
William Lucking	Thomas
Hrothgar Matthews	Art Nesbitt
Dawn Madsen	Leslie
Natassia Malthe	New Leslie
Eric Olsen	Mel
Derek Hamilton	New Mel
Doug Abrahams	Kent
Carrie Davis	Anne
Crystal Cass	New Anne
Peg Christopherson	Sylvie
Jaclynn Grad	New Sylvie
Barry Greene	Mark
Malcolm Stewart	Vic
Dorion Davis	Sherrie
Rafe McDonald	Tim
Barbara Howard	Karen
Michael Sunczyk	Red Robe
Laurel Gray	The Pathologist
Jon Ratt	The Husband
Tyler Labine	Gavin
Jenny Mitchell	Kim
Michael Buie	Randy
Kelly Irving	Ron
Fawnia L Mondey	Laurie

Death Toll:	3 females – drug overdose 2 males – both by drug overdose, one a suicide

CASE HISTORY:

THE WELL-PLANNED CRIME SCENE

Walter Condy once claimed that: 'What passes between you and your victim is the most intimate relationship possible for any two people. I know, some people think sex and all that is the closest two people can get, but it's not, not by a long shot. When you look into their dying eyes, they're not thinking about husbands or children, not even God. It's you and it's them. There's not another soul in the universe beside you two. How can't that leave an impression on a man, on what he does, what he thinks? You take away their lives, but they're still there, you know? They live on, through you. After that kind of intimacy, sex is ... sex is nothing. But, everything you do after a killing is part of them too.'

Condy's view of murder, romanticized so far from the brutal reality of his crimes that it almost became a religion to him, probably explains the bizarre scenarios police ran into when investigating the deaths of seven young men and women in the spring of 1967. Police frequently encounter staging, the deliberate alteration of a crime scene, but they'd never seen anything quite like Condy's work in the small community of Rochester. Then-Detective Giles Marley recalls, 'The previous summer, a young woman committed suicide in her bathtub and, before we could arrive at the scene, her distraught boyfriend had washed off all the blood, wrapped her in a dressing gown to hide her nudity, and begun blow-drying her hair. He didn't want "anyone seeing her like that". So, yes, we expect crime scenes to be altered from time to time. In some cases, like that suicide, we almost expect it. Condy's staging, however, was the most elaborate we'd ever heard of.'

Condy's first scene, if it hadn't happened twenty-eight years before *Millennium* was even a twinkle in Chris Carter's eye, could have been lifted right out of 'Loin Like A Hunting Flame'. A young couple, drugged, then strangled with wide, soft, ligatures so as to leave as few marks as possible, were found in the Rochester Public Gardens just after the crocuses pushed their way up and the new public viewing season began. With nothing more than edible grape leaves from a specialty groceteria to cover their genitalia, and apples held in their hands by rubber-bands, Connie Levin and Pakash Remi were found by gardeners mulching the flower beds. 'I looked at this scene for a good five minutes before it really sank in that they were dead,' Marley remembers. 'If you've ever seen kids dressed up at Christmas as The Wise Men and all the rest, you know exactly what we saw. Except, Connie and Pakash weren't acting.'

Autopsy results strongly suggested Connie Levin was a virgin the night she and Pakash were abducted. Oddly enough, though Condy readily admits killing the couple, and pubic hairs matching Condy's were combed from Connie's body, he repeatedly denies having any sexual contact with her, or any of his other victims.

CATCH IT? The lead local investigator of this episode is named Thomas. The odd title of this episode is from an equally-odd poem entitled 'The Ballad of the Long-Legged Bait' by Dylan *Thomas*.

His next victim, Catherine Faye Gerherty, had been jogging when she disappeared three weeks later. Her naked body, also strangled, though not sexually assaulted, was prostrated before a makeshift cross of two boughs taken from the pine trees where she was found. The posture, face down with arms extended to either side, strongly evocative of a priest during sacring, hid her face, breasts and pubic area from casual view. Police, after documenting the scene and removing the body, discovered one of Connie Levin's earrings pressed into the ground below.

When Frank Black describes Arthur Nesbitt's posing and staging of the crime scenes as 'a window into sexuality, what he wants it to be, perfect, uninhibited, guiltless' he could as easily have been describing Condy's fantasies about murder. Nesbitt experienced all the sexual activity he missed previously by watching others. Condy wanted the police to realize that he wasn't really killing people, he was consummating a 'deeper relationship'. In interviews after capture, he explained how nothing, not original sin, not a religious conviction, not anything could possibly be 'closer' than his 'rela-

tionship' with the vic-
tims. To Condy, by shar-
ing 'their last breaths',
those last few moments
of life, he and his victims
accomplished a ritualis-
tic style of 'soul-mar-
riage'. He honestly
believed that their souls
remained tied to him in
some mystical way that
defied time or place.

His one other male
victim, Patrick Cooper,
picked up his long-time
girl, Katie Dwyer for a
night at the movies, but
never brought her home.
Two days later, their
bodies were found in the
same small wooded area
where Catherine Faye
Gerherty was discov-
ered. Just off a public
walking path, Katie sat

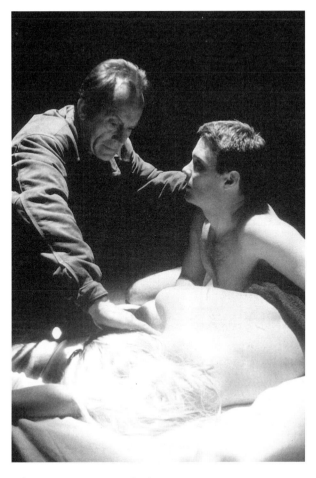

with her back propped against a tree. Her clothes were
neatly and modestly arranged, but her hands had been
bound together with duct tape. Completely naked, Patrick
Cooper was propped in the circle of her arms, his head
resting against hers. Though Condy exhibited great reluctance to discuss any of his male victims, psychologists on his
case speculate the scene recreates as nearly as possible some
variation of a mother-child scenario, maybe even the
Madonna with Child print found in Condy's apartment
after his arrest.

THE SEXUALLY-
VIOLENT THEMES
SIMMERING SINCE
'THE PILOT' EXPLODE
IN 'LOIN LIKE A
HUNTING FLAME'

What the fictional Arthur Nesbitt shares with real-life
killer Walter Condy, and any of the other multitude of delusional killers, is the inability to truly separate fantasy from
acceptable daily behavior. The problem isn't unique to murderers either. For some time, a subclass of rapist has been

recognized by criminal investigators. This rapist uses just enough force to get what he wants, no more. He's likely to ask if the victim is 'comfortable' several times during the rape itself. He'll exhibit concern that she 'enjoy herself too'. If he knows the victim's address or phone number, he may even call to see 'what she's doing Saturday night'. So far removed from reality is this man that he's been known to give out his name and address so they can arrange another 'date'! Like Arthur Nesbitt, who finally felt married after fulfilling his video fantasy, who couldn't understand why anyone would question him, and who calmly returned to his own home as if nothing was wrong, the fantasy or delusional criminal frequently uses his crimes to act out the images in his head – often, the killing is an unfortunate incidental.

NOTEBOOK:

Getting Back To Basics

If anything was likely to strike viewers of this episode as odd – other than the realistic portrayal of events few of us really comprehend in the first place – it was Det. Thomas's stubborn refusal to agree to any description of the killer.

TESTIMONY TRIVIA 12

1 What won't be found in Boulder's biological garden?
2 Where did Det. Thomas work prior to moving to Boulder?
3 At what sort of party did Arthur play Peeping Tom?
4 Where were the honeymooners headed before being abducted?
5 What was Arthur Nesbitts' legitimate job?
6 What did Frank find in the Nesbitts' toilet?
7 Where was Arthur's makeshift 'studio' hidden?
8 How long had Karen and Arthur been married?
9 Where did Nesbitt pose the two dead women?
10 What did Maureen Murphy speculate set off Nesbitt's killing spree?

Sure, he was having problems of his own, but after years spent in sex crime investigation, forgetting the basics of criminal behavior seems as unlikely as 'un' learning how to ride a bike! Maybe he'll put a cheat-sheet in his pocket from now on, one very much like this one, which highlights the activities and characteristics of the two major classifications in determining suspect likelihood, the organization or disorganization of the killer and his crime scene.

Needless to say, Arthur Nesbitt falls into the 'organized' category. Even with all the horror worked into 'Loin Like A Hunting Flame', the scariest thing of all was still Nesbitt's closet!

INCIDENTALS:

Chris Carter and the Fox network are clearly believers in the maxim 'If something works, use it again – and again'! If, after this episode was over, you were left scratching your head and wondering just where you'd seen that guy hawking the club flyers before, you're obviously an X-Phile as well as a *Millen-*

THE ADDITION OF MAUREEN MURPHY (HARRIET SANSOM) TO THE GROUP REINFORCES THE 'MATURITY' OF THE MAIN CHARACTERS. THOUGH SOME VIEWERS THOUGHT A YOUNGER ELEMENT MIGHT ADD TO THE SHOW'S APPEAL, GROUP MEMBERS LIKE PETER WATTS (TERRY O'QUINN), PICTURED HERE IN 'GEHENNA', ARE QUICKLY GATHERING THEIR OWN ADMIRERS... MANY OF THEM IN THE YOUNGER DEMOGRAPHIC RANGE

ANSWERS

1 An apple tree
2 Los Angeles
3 A swing party, a wife-swapping party
4 Bali
5 He was a pharmacist
6 A 'smut' magazine that dated back to 1978
7 A forgotten bunker reached by a tunnel under the garage
8 Eighteen years
9 On a park bench
10 His upcoming anniversary

YOUR SCORE:

nium fan. That particular actor was 'Stoner' in two episodes of *The X-Files*. He smoked cockroach-infested dung in 'War of the Coprophages' and licked toads in 'Quagmire'. With the addition of Harriet Sansom (who portrayed the adult Eve in *The X-Files* episode of the same name) and Hrothgar Matthews (another alumnus of *XFU*), Carter and crew must have felt like it was 'Old Home Week'.

FROM CRIME SCENE TO PROFILE

The Organized Killer

Pre-Crime Characteristics

- Well-educated, higher IQ
- Able to maintain a job
- Is married, in relationship

- Meticulous, controlled
- Socially competent
- Stable childhood home
- Average/Good relationships with both parents
- Travels
- Erudite, out-going, amiable
- Drives late-model vehicle

Criminal Style

- Detailed planner
- Prefers stranger killings

The Disorganized Killer

Pre-Crime Characteristics

- Lower IQ
- Switches jobs often
- Seldom manages relationships
- Moody, often bi-polar
- Social misfit
- Difficult childhood
- Lop-sided relationships with either/both parents
- Stays close to home
- Withdrawn, may stammer
- Lacks personal hygiene
- Nocturnal
- Moves frequently

Criminal Style

- Spontaneous criminal
- Prefers family/ neighbors

- Aggressive killer
- Leaves little evidence
- Unlikely to converse
- Removes weapons
- Removes/hides body
- Ties/binds victim

- Sophisticated fantasies
- Maintains home in remote location
- Elaborate staging

- 'Blitz' attacks
- Ignores chaotic scene
- May chat-up victim
- Leaves weapons
- Dumps body at scene
- Leaves victims unrestrained

- May be necrophilic

Post-crime behaviors

- Returns to scene
- Follows media coverage
- Police freak
- Calm under questioning
- May move body several times
- Inserts self into criminal investigation
- Engages in elaborate contact with police investigators

Post-crime behaviors

- Returns to scene
- Ignores media coverage
- Attends funerals
- Moves after crime
- Behavior changes
- May confess while under the influence or write incriminating diaries/ poems

▶ ▶ ▶ ▶ ▶ ▶

THE 'MILLENNIUM' QUOTATIONS

Chris Carter has become well-known for combining the seemingly incompatible. Aliens, sexual tension, and the FBI in *The X-Files*. Prophecy, poetry, and serial killers in *Millennium*. It's a combination that seems to be working, adding yet another layer of depth to a program that's already addressing some pretty deep questions.

Oddly enough, what would soon become *Millennium*'s signature opening, the verses stark against their black backgrounds, was absent from the first episode. Not that 'The Pilot' was lacking in poetry. Between Yeats and Nostradamus, it had more than all the others put together.

'The Pilot'

BEEN THERE, DONE THAT

It's not only modern forty-somethings that contemplate the deplorable state of the world around them. Chris Carter created *Millennium*; Yeats wrote *The Second Coming*, which Frank Black's first television adversary would quote some three-quarters of a century later.

THE SECOND COMING

Turning and turning in the widening gyre

The falcon cannot hear the falconer;

Things fall apart; the centre cannot hold;

Mere anarchy is loosed upon the world,

The blood-dimmed tide is loosed, and everywhere

The ceremony of innocence is drowned;

The best lack all conviction, while the worst

Are full of passionate intensity.

Surely some revelation is at hand;

Surely the Second Coming is at hand.

The Second Coming! Hardly are those words out

When a vast image out of Spiritus Mundi

Troubles my sight; somewhere in sands of the desert

A shape with lion body and the head of a man,

A gaze bland and pitiless as the sun,

Is moving its slow thighs, while all about it

Reel shadows of the indignant desert birds.

The darkness drops again; but now I know

That twenty centuries of stony sleep

Were vexed to nightmare by a rocking cradle,

And what rough beast, its hour come round at last,

Slouches towards Bethlehem to be born?

WILLIAM BUTLER YEATS, 1920

Disillusioned by the seemingly endless civil hardships in his native Ireland – Yeats lost several close acquaintances during the Easter uprising the previous year and later watched Britain 'renege' on an agreement that would have given Ireland independence – he truly felt he was living in the fading days of some historically significant era. Influenced by studies of occultism (he was a member of both 'The Theosophical Society's Esoteric Branch' and 'The Golden Dawn'), Tibet's mystic theology, Buddhism, Egyptology, and, of course, biblical (he was the grandson of an Orthodox rector of the Church of England), he believed he would see the end of a great two thousand year cycle in his own lifetime.

'Gehenna'

A contemporary of Yeats' provided the quote from 'Gehenna'.

BLESSED EVENT

Round the three actors in any blessed event
Is always standing an invisible audience of four,
The double twins, the fallen natures of man.

On the Left they remember difficult childhoods,
On the Right they have forgotten why they were so happy,
Above sit the best decisive people,
Below they must kneel all day so as not to be governed.

Four voices just audible in the hush of any Christmas:
Accept my friendship or die.
I shall keep order and not very much will happen.
Bring me luck and of course I'll support you.
I smell blood and an era of prominent madmen.

But the Three hear nothing and are blind even to the
landscape
With its towns and rivers and pretty pieces of nonsense.

He, all father, repenting their animal nights,

Cries: Why did She have to be tortured? It is all my fault.

Once more a virgin, She whispers: The Future shall never
  suffer.

And the New Life awkwardly touches its home, beginning
  to fumble

About in the Truth for the straight successful Way

Which will always appear to end in some dreadful defeat.

W H AUDEN, NOVEMBER 1939

Like most young men, Auden bucked the system a bit, attaching himself to the radical left and proposing major changes in the status quo. Though those messages grew more tempered as Auden's view of the world matured, he never lost the deep-seated belief that individuals made significant changes in their societies – as long as they *chose* to act.

'Dead Letters'

Somewhat oddly, *Millennium* began incorporating biblical quotes in one of the episodes most removed from the 'millennial' influences underlying the program. Still, considering that most of the millennial thinking evolved from biblical prophesy, it had to start somewhere.

'For the thing that I have greatly feared has come upon me. And what I have dreaded has happened to me. I am not at ease, nor am I quiet; I have no rest for trouble comes.'

JOB 3:25,26

'The Judge'

Though Herman Melville's *Moby Dick* wasn't really recognized in literary circles during his lifetime, he was a relatively prolific writer, penning five popular successes before *Moby Dick* and continuing to make gains with many of his short stories. However, obscure or not, many of his works share something in common with *Millennium*. Just as Ten-Thirteen and Fox discovered when their ratings nose-dived almost from the start, it takes time to build an audience when the subject matter is dark and self-exploratory. Both *Moby Dick* and Melville's next book, *Pierre: Or the Ambiguities*, an even darker tale on the nature of evil, were financial flops. However, also like *Millennium* Melville's themes focused on a then-modern view of the world. In shorts like *Benito Cereno* which addressed the issue of slavery in parable form, Melville frequently castigated his society for allowing the descent into anarchy. Melville, like Carter, described his work as 'a basic conflict between good and evil'.

The quotation used in this episode didn't come from one of his lesser known works, however, but from *Moby Dick* as the narrator contemplates the differences between his perception and that of his companions, and between him and the animal world.

'Though neither knows where lie the nameless things of which the mystic sign gives forth such hints; yet with me, as with the colt, somewhere those things must exist. Though in many of its aspects this visible world seems formed in love, the invisible spheres were formed in fright.'

HERMAN MELVILLE, *Moby Dick*

'522666'

Only the crew at Ten-Thirteen could mix poetic quotations with terrorism, though in this case, the connection was certainly appropriate.

> 'I am responsible for everything …
> except my very responsibility.'
>
> JEAN-PAUL SARTRE

Sartre was an existentialist and among the beliefs that his writing so accurately reflected was his atheism. He firmly believed in society's, and the individual's, ethical responsibility to involve themselves in the social and political activities of their time. While he wasn't idealistic enough to believe that a man's destiny was totally within his grasp, in fact he frequently stated that man's powerlessness was inevitable, a part of the human condition, Sartre saw no reason why these two beliefs shouldn't be compatible. Just because the individual was incapable of changing destiny alone was no reason for him to stop trying. He adhered to the notion that enough individuals *were* the society and that the reason society was limping along so badly was that not all its members were keeping up!

'Kingdom Come'

> 'And there will be such darkness,
> that one can feel it.'
>
> EXODUS 10:21

Exodus is not, in any sense, part of those books of the Bible that together make up the Apocrypha, but it might well have seemed like the end of the world to the Egyptians. The 'darkness' of Exodus 10:21 was one God ordered Moses to bring down on the Egyptians who hadn't quite decided to let the Israelites leave their enslavement.

'Blood Relatives'

While most biblical passages seem to have numerous meanings, some even appearing contradictory, this passage from Luke is a curious choice for *Millennium*. The passage quoted, 'This generation is a wicked generation; it seeks for a sign, and yet no sign shall be given to it ...' actually ends with '...except the sign of Jonah'. According to Luke, Christ was berating those who were asking for miracles, implying that faith alone was sufficient. While perhaps appropriate to a religious figure, it's in complete opposition to everything the Millennium Group seems dedicated to accomplishing. They may not be looking for miracles, but they're certainly not content to assume the future takes care of itself. Far from it. One of the program's major themes is that the chaos growing around us just may not be random, and Frank's self-stated goal is to seek for all the signs he can find!

'The Well-Worn Lock'

Many of the authors, philosophers and poets featured in the *Millennium* opening quotes will be surprises to viewers. Few, for example, realize that Robert Louis Stevenson, famous for rip-roaring adventures like *The Strange Case of Dr Jekyll and Mr Hyde*, which could easily inspire a *Millennium* episode itself, *Treasure Island*, *Kidnapped*, and *The Master of Ballantrae*, was also a skilled writer of essays and literary criticism! The quote used in this episode, 'The cruelest lies are often told in silence' is from *Virginibus Puerisque*, a collection of essays written by Stevenson in 1881.

'Wide Open'

For their second quote from the Book of Job, the *Millennium* production team chose 5:4, 'His children are far from safety; they shall be crushed at the gate without a rescuer.' Real doomsday stuff, but, historically speaking, the events depicted in Job occurred during a period of great hardship and chaos.

'The Wild And The Innocent'

'O Lord, if there is a Lord,
Save my soul, if I have a soul—'

ERNEST JOSEPH RENAN

It's said that there's no firmer non-smoker than a reformed smoker, no stauncher believer than a convert, and no greater atheist than an ex-priest. Ernest Renan trained as a Roman Catholic priest, but broke off relations with his faith to write widely, and controversially, on the historical and philosophical aspects of Christianity as well Judaism. This particular quote comes from *The Skeptic's Prayer*.

'Weeds'

'But know ye for certain … Ye shall surely
bring innocent blood upon yourselves
and upon this city …'

JEREMIAH 26:13

Unlike Job, Jeremiah is firmly camped in the Prophets section of the Old Testament and is more organized than many of the poetic or narrative books. The first section, chapters 1-25, consists of prophecies spoken by Jeremiah – in the first person – against Judah and Jerusalem. The next section, 26–45 tells Jeremiah's story, his actions, the trials he faced and the persecution he endured until his death. Chapter 26, the source of this episode's quote, records his life under King Jehoiakim. The last section of Jeremiah are the prophet's visions of Jerusalem's neighbors, a particularly unpleasant set of images. Jeremiah is practically unique among the biblical prophets in that he was alone during his visionary period. The last prophet before him, Isaiah, was dead nearly three-quarters of a century before Jeremiah took up the trade and it would be several decades after his murder before anyone else continued the tradition.

'Loin Like A Hunting Flame'

The production company not only included a quote in this episode, but pulled the title from poetry as well. In a poem with the curious title 'The Ballad of the Long-Legged Bait', Dylan Thomas evoked equally curious images like:

> *Good-bye to chimneys and funnels,*
> *Old wives that spin in the smoke,*
> *He was blind to the eyes of candles*
> *In the praying windows of waves ...*

To say Thomas's poetry includes a considerable measure of personal fantasy, and a heavy dose of surrealism would be just scratching at a description of the welshman's style. It certainly makes one wonder what was going through the production team's collective mind when they picked a line nearly four pages into Thomas's six-page poem from this qua-train:

And steeples pierce the could on her shoulder

And the streets that the fisherman combed

When his long-legged flesh was a wind on fire

And his loin was a hunting flame.

In an episode about a man with a secret fantasy life, the black and white quote 'Two souls, alas, are housed within my breast' makes literary and symbolic sense. That the quote comes from Johann Wolfgang von Goethe's *Faust*, the tale of a medieval scholar-magician leaves other resonances in its wake. The allusion to Arthur Nesbitt's double life is obvious, but what else would Frank Black himself have been called in the Middle Ages? And, caught between his need to protect his family, and his responsibilities to his community and the Millennium Group, it's certain that he, too, often feels torn, as if two souls were housed in one body.

TESTIMONY TRIVIA SCORECARD

Well, you made it to the end. If you've kept a running tally of your points, we'll see just how good an observer you really are.

0–29   Remember that Alzheimer patient we mentioned in the Trivia intro way back in Chapter One? Probably not if you couldn't answer more than 30 questions out of 142! Warm up the VCR. You'll need some review work before you could be a credible witness, much less a member of the Millennium Group!

30–59   Okay, so you're not an Alzheimer patient. Actually, if you managed to score anything between 40 and 60, you're dead average for the general real world population. Stats tell us that if 10 people witnessed a car crash, only two of them would be able to accurately remember the colour of the car after 48 hours. Still, training can improve your observation technique so dig out those tapes and see how many details you catch this time.

60–89   Hey, you and Geibelhouse should get along just fine! He always was a step or two behind Bletch, who, of course, was a step or two behind Frank and his colleagues ... But then again, who *isn't* playing catchup where the Millennium Group is concerned?

90–119   You know, you've got potential ... But so did James Horn. Why not get yourself a mental health medical, pick up some stock in Tums or Mylanta, and drop a résumé by the office? Don't know where the office is? Then try 1910 Ezekiel in Seattle.

120–142   The Millennium Group wants you!

Of course, you *do* have a chance to improve your overall scores. Volume II of *The Unofficial Millennium Companion* will be out in a few months with trivia busters for the remaining 12 episodes of Season One.

On the other hand, if you're willing to accept your limitations, concede that you're not even up to Geibelhouse's standard of observation, you can do what so many others do and, with the help of your VCR, turn the trivia busters into your own customized drinking game. The rules are simple.

1 Have plenty of brew on hand (or gummy bears if you're a teetotaller).
2 Read the questions *before* starting the tape or watching the episode on broadcast television if you're already in reruns.
3 First person to find the answer to a question during the program takes a gulp or munches a gummy. Last person to catch the answer takes two gulps or two gummies.

Good Luck!

PHOTOGRAPHIC ACKNOWLEDGEMENTS

Grateful acknowledgement is made for permission to reprint the following photographs:

Pages 17, 24,33,55, 59, 80, 127 © Fox Broadcasting Company/ courtesy of Photofest

Page 81 © 20th Century Fox/courtesy of Photofest

Pages 10, 15, 29, 47, 51, 63, 72, 78, 79, 98, 107, 111, 125 © Fox Broadcasting Company/courtesy of the Everett Collection

Page 82 © Warner Brothers/courtesy of Photofest

Page 9 © Steve Labadessa/Outline

Page 74 © Karen Moskowitz/Outline

ABOUT THE AUTHOR

N. E. GENGE lives and works out of the far reaches of northern Canada. She is a documentary scriptwriter as well as the author of two historical biographies, and a regular contributor to publications such as *The Times*. Her fiction has appeared in *Aboriginal Science Fiction*, *Asimov's Science Fiction* and *Story*. As the author of *The Unofficial X-Files Companion* and *The New Unofficial X-Files Companion*, she is something of an expert on Chris Carter's creations.

THE UNOFFICIAL

Millennium

Companion

THE COVERT CASEBOOK
OF THE
MILLENNIUM GROUP

VOLUME TWO

The end of the millennium approaches ...

Cults rise and fall, criminal psychotics find new causes, and 'end times' terror intrudes even into the precincts of the Yellow House. Against the madness stands the mysterious Millennium Group, its most 'insightful' investigator, Frank Black, and his family, who may see more than even Black realizes.

Volume Two of *The Unofficial Millennium Companion* digs even deeper into the dark world where criminals and their profilers discover just how much they have common ... how deep inside the Killer's mind his Hunter must delve.

The essential companion to Volume One, this book includes some terrifying revelations.

- which portents and prophecies have been fulfilled and what predictions wait in the wings for their turn?
- what is the criminal subculture? How does jail foster it? What sort of criminal does it put back on our streets?
- what could Frank Black learn from the real criminal profilers?
- background information on the real-life events threaded through every episode
- photos and annotated maps of the Millennium Group's travels
- and just who are the members of the Millennium Group?